Nov. 1991

Ozark Tall Tales

Ozark Tall Tales

Collected from the Oral Tradition

By Richard and Judy Dockrey Young

August House / *Little Rock*

P U B L I S H E R S

Published by August House, Inc.,
P.O. Box 3223, Little Rock, Arkansas, 72203,
501-663-7300.

Printed in the United States of America

10 9 8 7 6 5 4 3 2 1

LIBRARY OF CONGRESS CATALOGING-IN-PUBLICATION DATA

Ozark tall tales : collected from the oral tradition / edited by
Richard and Judy Dockrey Young. — 1st ed.
    p.   cm.
Includes index.
ISBN 0-87483-099-0 : $8.95
1. Tall tales—Ozark Mountains Region. 2. Folklore—Ozark
Mountains Region.
  I. Young, Richard, 1946-   . II. Young, Judy Dockrey, 1949-   .
GR110.M77094   1989
398.2'097671—dc20   89-35858
                                           CIP

First Edition, 1989

Cover illustration by Wendell E. Hall
Production artwork by Ira Hocut
Typography by Lettergraphics, Memphis, Tennessee
Design direction by Ted Parkhurst
Project direction by Hope Coulter

This book is printed on archival-quality paper which meets the
guidelines for performance and durability of the Committee on
Production Guidelines for Book Longevity of the Council on
Library Resources.

AUGUST HOUSE, INC.   PUBLISHERS   LITTLE ROCK

This book is dedicated to the memory of

Morgan Martin Young, Ed.D.
November 27, 1902–November 13, 1982

for the stories he told.

Contents

Introduction

The Ozark Plateau stretches from eastern Okla-
homa, northward by way of its Kiamichi Mountains and
Cookson Hills into southeastern Kansas, across central
Missouri south of the Missouri River, into southwestern
Illinois, southward along the western side of the Missis-
sippi River Valley, and across Arkansas north of the
Arkansas River, lapping across that river south into the
Ouachita Mountains to our original starting point. Within
those rough boundaries there still exists a pace of life
reminiscent of earlier times in America. There are radios
and cassette players in cars and pleasure boats, televisions
and VCRs in the houses and cabins, satellite dishes in the
yards; but around campfires and fireplaces and candles,
the art of storytelling is alive and well, and rivals the
modern entertainments.

Many stories came from Europe, especially Great Brit-
ain, and mostly by way of the Appalachians, with many
embellishments based on hill life. Other stories sprang
from real experiences in a wild and isolated part of
America—stories of hunting, of adventures with animals,
and of strange places. Still others grow and bloom in the
fertile imagination and gentle humor of the Ozark folks.
As we have lived and worked in these Ozark hills, folks
have shared their stories with us and we in turn pass them

along to you. All the tales in this collection are in the public domain, many of them over a century old; some are quite recent and entering print for the first time. How we came by them is a tale in itself.

We both come from families where stories were told and read at bedtime and around the fire. We are both part of the last generation to grow up before the advent and wide-spread popularity of portable, battery-operated radios and cassette recorders made more personal forms of amusement seem obsolete. We both come from hill families: Judy from the hills of eastern Oklahoma, Richard from the hill country of east central Texas. We have both heard and enjoyed stories all our lives and began seriously collecting early: Richard in 1968 and Judy in 1978.

Ozark stories have persevered because the Ozark way of life has endured with far less change than in urban areas. More folks know and tell stories in the Ozarks, which has made it easier for us to hear and learn these tales exclusively by word of mouth, instead of from literary sources. We have both worked as professional storytellers, especially in Midwestern parks and theme parks, and have picked up all the yarns in this collection by trading with "locals" and "come-heres." Even the flatlanders tell us stories—but they belong in a different anthology.

The main body of this work was collected between 1981 and 1988. Most of our stories were told to us by white males between the ages of sixteen and sixty-five; they are the traditional tellers in Ozark society. (Vance Randolph, in his introduction to *We Always Lie to Strangers*, points out that men tell the tall tales, while women tell folklore and superstitions.) Among the menfolk, young men aged sixteen to thirty tend to tell hunting stories, outlaw tales, and jokes; men thirty to fifty tell "lies" and stories about how foolish some other man is; men fifty and older retell stories from their childhood to their grandchildren, and pass along legends and lore of their heritage. We have included an index of informants after the stories, to give the reader more insight into the background of the tales.

In the course of preparing this manuscript, we received invaluable assistance from Janet Watkins and Dennis VanArsdale in reference research; from Jim Moeskau, who encouraged the writing of this book; from Scooter Huddleston, who helped sort and arrange these stories; and from our families, who did all the usual wonderful family-type things. To them, and to the folks at August House, we extend our heartfelt thanks. Any flaws in the work are ours, not theirs.

Last of all, but most of all, we thank the hundreds of good Ozark folks who joined with us in the timeless ritual that is humanity's oldest: the art and craft of storytelling.

JUDY DOCKREY YOUNG AND
RICHARD ALAN YOUNG
Harrison, Arkansas
1989

Notes on Ozark Dialect

Many scholarly studies of the Ozark dialect have been conducted, but as modern communications reach deep into the hills, and video rental stores and satellite dishes appear in Ozark towns, the dialect is changing and fading. Many of the peculiarities observed by noted folklorists Vance Randolph in Missouri and Otto Earnest Rayburn in Arkansas during the 1930s have disappeared. "Pure" Ozark dialect is being mixed with standard English and midwestern dialect so that, for example, the "pure" Ozark *you-uns* is heard less often now than the midwestern or generic southern *y'all.* Many regionalisms (e.g., *to bobble* for *to err*), archaisms (e.g., *budget* for *pouch*), and euphemisms (e.g., *limb* for the presumably more sensual *leg*) are used "more by the ol' folks."

Still, many traces of the older, often more Elizabethan-sounding, dialect can be heard in the Ozarks.

Some words have changed meaning here. *Proud* means *happy,* and *prideful* replaces *proud.* Some words have slightly altered pronunciations—*tush* for *tusk, painter* for *panther, ballit* for *ballad,* and so on. Some suffixes have altered pronunciation: words ending in *-ow* become *-er* (*window = windder, swallow = swaller*), words ending in *-ash* become *-arsh* (wash = warsh, squash = squarsh). And some words undergo vowel shifts, as in *fit* for *fought, jist*

15

for *just*, and *whup* for *whip*. The direction of the shift (low vowel to middle, middle vowel to high, and so on) is not always predictable.

Metathesis—or the transposition of sounds, as when *pretty* becomes *purty*—sometimes occurs, just as it did in Anglo-Saxon (for instance, *waesp* becoming *waeps*). Some vowels shift with predictability, as when the sound *-er* becomes *-ar* (*bear* = *b'ar*, *perilous* = *par'lous*). There is also occasional consonant shift, especially among the nasals and linguapalatals, as in *chimley* for *chimney*, and the borrowed midwestern *idn't* for *isn't* and *wadn't* for *wasn't*. Frequently, consonant combinations are reduced to simpler pronunciations: *crumble* reduces to *crum'le*, *shrimp* becomes *s'rimp*, and so on. There is even reverse correction, when the speaker "puts back in" sounds that he assumes have been carelessly omitted, as in *fambly* for *family* or the humorous *'taters an' turnips* becoming *potaters an' poternips*.

Among verbs, those ending in *-led* are usually pronounced *-lt* (*boiled* = *b'ilt*, *spilled* = *spilt*, *killed* = *kilt*). Verbs with the internal sound *-oi-* reduce to long *i* (*boil* = *b'il*, which sounds like *bile*; *hoist* = *h'ist*, which sounds like *heist*; *roil* = *r'ile*, which sounds like *rile*).

Past participles often replace the simple past tense forms ("he taken" for "he took"), and some archaic past participles and past tenses are retained (*wrought*, *woken*, *et*, for example).

Where midwestern dialect influences Ozark speech, some *l*'s disappear (*himse'f*, *he'p*, *she'f*), and final *-ow* becomes *-uh* (*window* = *windo'* = *winduh*, *follow* = *follo'* = *folluh*) instead of the more purely Ozark *-er*.

Finally, the particles in Ozark speech tend to reduce to the schwa with the minimum of consonants (as in *for* = *fuhr* = *fuh,'* *to* = *tuh* = *'uh*, *of* = *uhv* = *uh.'* These are often spelled *fo,'* *'o*, and *o,'* respectively, in transcriptions, but never pronounced *foh* or *oh* when read aloud. *The* also

16

may become *thuh* = *th.*

In this book we have minimized phonetic spellings of the Ozark dialect in order to make the stories easier to read and enjoy. However, since the many tales we have heard through the years have come in all levels of dialect, from the most proper standard English to some wonderful hill speech that requires considerable explanation for the average flatlander, we have tried to retain in each story a level of dialect that represents its origin or the way it was told to us.

To truly appreciate these yarns, they must be read aloud—or better yet, told orally, as they were when they first came to us. The pronunciation and the dialect are less important than the charm of the stories themselves.

RICHARD ALAN YOUNG

Jack Tales

*The epics of Ozark tall tales, these
stories of the crafty but
good-hearted young hero came
to the Ozarks from England
via Appalachia.*

Jack and the Gowerow

1 **There's all kind of things that live in the** hollers and caves of the Ozarks—like williwaws, whompus cats, and whoofenpoofs—but the fearsomest critter of 'em all is the gowerow!

Now, the gowerow is big, mean, and ugly, like a cross between a razorback hog and a alligator, ten feet high and twenty feet long. Its feet've got big claws. It's got a long, humpy back with a row of spikes coming off it.[1] It's got a long tail with a whomper on the end of it that it can whomp you with. It's got this big long, ugly muzzle with one nostril in the end of it, and one spikey horn on the top of its nose. It's got four eyes that glow like coals and two long tushes[2] a-dangling out of its mouth. And it eats what it wants, man or beast.

Some folks says there was a gowerow in Boone County,[3] but that's just foolishness. Most of 'em was down in Searcy County where they sometimes ran for sheriff—and got elected. But there was one gowerow lived in a cave in a bluff not far from Boone County, overlooking a settlement. He come to consider that that town was his personal property, so that onc't a week, when he got hungry, or when he'd digested, he'd come a-tromping down into the town and grab him up a pig or a mule, or sometimes a cow or a horse! And he'd take 'em back up to the cave and eat 'em.

21

Now, the folks in this town was prosperous; the bottom-land was good, and they could afford to lose some livestock now and again. But onc't a year, in the spring, the go-werow'd take a hankering for something human.

He'd come snarling and glowering out of that cave, tromping acrost the valley, till he'd found some dumb boy or girl that hadn't hid, and carry 'em back to the cave for vittles. The folks in the town was heart-broke, but they couldn't do nothing to stop him. They'd tried. They tried shooting him, but lead balls just bounced off his hide. They tried blowing him up with powder; they blowed up a perfectly good mule in the attempt; but it didn't hurt the gowerow at all. So most folks just hid their children in the spring, until the gowerow had caught a stupid one or a drifter somewheres, and left town.

Now, Jack, he was the smallest, brightest boy in his family,[4] and he set out to make his fortune in the world. He lived off his wits for a long spell, wandering and looking for a place to settle down. He come a-walking down the road into this town one spring day and up come a woman driving a wagon and a hitch of mules. She stopped and said to him, "Ain't you got a lick of sense? Get off'n the road and hide somewheres. The gowerow is a-coming!"

Now Jack, he didn't know what a gowerow was, being from out of state and all, so she h'isted him up on the wagon-seat and explained all about gowerows. "We just had to get out of town," she said, "or the gowerow might get our girl." At that, the pile of burlap bags in the wagon moved, and out looked the prettiest girl Jack had ever seen.

Jack turned on the seat and commenced to greet the girl polite-like. "Why," the girl said, "didn't you know the go-werow'd get you?"

"Pshaw," said Jack, "I ain't a-feared of no gowerow."

"You must be awful brave," said the girl.

"Why, I could kill that old gowerow," said Jack.

The man of the family was walking behind the wagon

with a rifle, and the girl's ma clucked at the mules and they commenced to move on. Jack and the girl talked a while, and Jack decided he wanted to marry this here girl. He jumped off and walked alongside the pa, and said, "Feller, I'd like to marry your daughter."

The feller laughed. "You're just a drifter!" he said.

"Ain't I good enough?" asked Jack. "What could I do to prove I'd be a good son?"

The feller kind of chuckled under his breath, and said, "Why, all you got to do is go to town and kill that gowerow. Then you can marry up with my daughter."

Jack said, "Have I got your word on that?"

The feller chuckled and said, "Why, sure!"

So Jack took off headed for town; didn't have the leastest idea how he was going to do it, but he was a-going to kill that gowerow.

When he come into the town, the place was all deserted. Every family with young'uns had up and left. He finally found four old men in the blacksmith shop. They figured they was too tough for gowerow meat. Up walks Jack and says, "Howdy, fellers, my name's Jack, and I'm going to kill the gowerow."

They laughed and laughed, just like the girl's daddy had done, all except for the old one-eyed blacksmith.

The blacksmith, he begun to quizzing Jack as to why he was feeling so suicidal, and Jack explained about the girl, and all. Now, when the other fellers had fell to talking amongst theirselves again, the smith, he says to Jack, "Come here, son, and let me show you something."

And he led him back behind the forge, to where he lived. The smith got under the rope bed in the corner, pulled out a long, skinny box, and creaked open the lid. He pulled out absolutely the biggest old double-barrel shotgun Jack'd ever seen. Them barrels was five foot long, and a inch acrost the bore. He handed the gun to Jack, and Jack nearly fell down; it was nearly a cannon!

"I forged that gun myself," said the smith. "But by itself it ain't no gowerow killer. It's got to be loaded—with this!" And he reached into that box again and pulled out a little box and set it on his knee. He opened up the little box, and drawed out these two iron arrows about eight inches long, all ground and shiny, with four blades crist-crost on the end.

"Now, these here is gowerow killers," said the smith, "made from the metal of a shooting star. I found it myself. I forged 'em myself. I put the spells on 'em myself. You want to kill a gowerow, them'll do it!"

"Why ain't you ever killt it?" asked Jack, h'isting the old gun up.

"One eye," said the smith. "And besides, I'm too blamed old."

Just then they heard it—roaring and snorting and spewing! The gowerow was a-coming!

They got the powder in just in time, and rammed them bolts in without no wadding. Out run Jack, past them old men, onto the path. There come the gowerow, its claws tearing up turf, breaking down fence-rows as it come. Jack backed up against a good-sized oak tree, knowing that gun'd kick like a new spring mule when he pulled the trigger. Backed his back up against it, and the old gowerow come a-scuffing along, not fifteen yards from Jack. But didn't see him.

Jack raised that old gun up and let fly the first bolt: *kawhoom!*[5] Right at the old gowerow's side. It knocked Jack down in spite of the tree.

The bolt hit the gowerow right in the ribs. Hurt him bad. He was limping as he turned and crawled at Jack. He'd never been hurt in his whole miserable life, and it made him madder'n fire. He's looking for somebody to bite! Jack's lying on the ground; seen that gowerow bearing down on him, slathering[6] and bleeding. He just managed to raise up that gun as the gowerow opened his mouth;

looked like a bushel basket full of spikes. Jack put the barrel in the gowerow's mouth and let fly that second bolt right down the critter's throat—*ka-whoom!*

It knocked Jack clean out, but it killed the gowerow. And when he quit a-thrashing about and hit the ground, his head was just about laying on Jack's foot.[7]

Them old men and the smith come a-tearing out of the forge and commenced to chopping on the old gowerow with axes, but ever'body knowed it was Jack and them shooting star arrows that had killed him.

Pretty soon Jack come to and shook his brains back in place, and took the smithy's axe, and he chopped and hacked and hewed that old gowerow's head clean off. The smith give him a burlap poke to carry it in, and Jack says, "I'm off to claim my prize!"

He took off up the road, the smith and the men with bloodied axes follering[8] him. They found the feller with the wagon, and you shoulda seen the look on that feller's face when Jack shook the bloody gowerow head out of that poke and said, "I've come to claim your daughter; there's the price!"

"Dad-gum!" said the feller. "I never intended to let you marry my daughter, even if you did kill the gowerow!"

Jack said, "I know you didn't; but you gived me your word."

The smith and the men from town commenced to reasoning with him. Said, "Come on, now, Hiram. We're going to give this boy all the cattle and pigs the thing would've et in a year."

'Nother said, "And a parcel of land to go with it!"

Smithy said, "And a plow, and all the tools he needs."

Jack said, "Now, feller, if'n you keep your word, we'll settle right here, and you can watch your grandkids grow."

Well, the old feller finally give in. He had to! And Jack done just what he said he'd do: he give up drifting and married that pretty girl, they raised a whole passel[9] of pretty children, but never again, in the spring, did they take the children out of town to hide 'em, to keep the gowerow from eating 'em up.

---

[1]The name *gower, gowerow,* or *gow-row* is derived from the Anglo-Saxon word *gar-raew,* meaning "row of spears," describing its spiked spine. To the editors' knowledge this fact has never entered print until now, although tales of gowerows have been collected extensively, from anecdotes by Ernie Deane to stories published by Vance Randolph. The association of the spiked spine with fierceness and savagery is found in the legend of the razorback hog as well. (See the reading list in the indexes.)

[2]Tusks.

[3]Boone County, Arkansas, was said to be the home of a gowerow, first described over a century ago, according to Deane. Randolph notes that a "gowrow" was killed near Marshall, Arkansas, in the 1890s, according to the locals.

[4]Jack, which implies both small and male in Anglo-Saxon, is always the youngest son.

[5]One would not think that such a simple thing as the onomatopoeic *ka-whoom* could be debated, but some historians say that *ka-* shows the percussion cap going off, or the explosion at the fire-hole, preceding the *whoom* emanating from the barrel, indicating the age of the story. Others propose that the *ka-* is phonetically the same as the Anglo-Saxon prefix *ge-,* which implies past participle, and is sounded appropriately before words ending in *-n* or *-m.*

[6]A variant of *slavering,* apparently caused by confusion with *lathering,* a term describing the sweating-up of horses.

[7]For the gowerow's head to lie at Jack's feet is an archetypal symbol of submission, which would prove beyond doubt that it was indeed Jack who had killed it. Without this important element, the knowledgeable audience might think the axes had, in fact, dealt the death blows.

[8]Following. The troop of now-loyal men accompanying Jack to claim his prize is another archetype. Without the presence of these men, the father would have had no proof of Jack's being the killer of the gowerow. The loyal, rescued horde is also an important folk motif.

[9]Parcel, implying a large number. Pronounced also as *pessel.* It is interesting that in the version retold here one informant used *parcel* correctly in reference to land, presumably because of "citified" influence at the court-house or land office.

This is perhaps the finest Jack tale told in the Ozarks, especially in Arkansas and Missouri. No single informant could be associated with this tale, as the editors have heard fragments and versions of it too many times to count. It has been heard as early as 1915 by Informant 36, and much more recently by Informants 22 and 24. All say they heard it from "the old folks."

Jack and Old Tush[1]

2 **Long ago, down on the hills and ridges,** near the little town of Omaha,[2] there lived three brothers. Now, the oldest one, his name was Will, the middle 'un was named Tom, and the youngest 'un was named Jack. But, having no womenfolks in the house, they taken turn-about fixing the supper.

One night it was Will's turn to fix the dinner, and he'd done purty good, boiled some beans 'n' ham, fried him up some 'taters. He stepped out on the porch when the vittles was ready, and picked up the iron rod and whanged on the dinner-bell a few times. Out from behind the house jumped this funny-looking feller; great big, lanky thing, only had one long tush right smack in the middle of his mouth! Had a bucket in his hand. He jumped out and come a-hubbing it[3] to the door, hollering, "Supper's ready; supper's ready; going to get cold!" He run up the stoop, run past Will faster'n a skip rock,[4] grabbed up all the supper, flung it in the bucket, and run out the door. He disappeart down the path a-fore Will could blink twic't. By the time Tom and Jack got to the house, they was[5] nothing to eat. Will explained it all, but they found it hard to swaller.[6] They got by on rinds and crusts[7] that night.

The next night it fell to Tom to cook the meal. He cut up cabbage and calf-steak, figuring to make up for the night a-

29

fore. He hadn't rung that dinner-bell but onc't when out come the old man loping up, hollering "Supper's ready! Supper's ready! Going to get cold!" and packing[8] that-there bucket; he swung the meal into it fast, and was out the door a-knocking Tom a-sprawling. He was gone in a twinkling. Clean disappeared, down in the holler. When Will and Jack got there, Tom was up and dusted off, a little addled, and told what'd happened. They made do on calf bones and cabbage stalk that night.

When it was Jack's turn, the next night, he wrung a chicken's neck and fried it up; made 'taters and gravy, and b'iled some greens. Then he taken all that good food and covered the pans with dishrags, and set it all in the kitchen safe.[9] What he put out on the table was some old dry cornbread from the week a-fore, and a pitcher of blinky.[10] Then he rung that dinner-bell to beat fire. Sure enough, here come Old Tush. "Supper's ready! Supper's ready! Going to get cold!" Jack stepped clean outen his way, and the old feller taken all that hardbread and all that blinky, and lit a shuck out down the holler. Jack, he taken the supper outen the safe, set it on the table, and slipping around from tree to tree, he follered Old Tush to the seep.[11] When Will and Tom come home, they et like kings.

Now, that Old Tush could run! He purt nigh flew down that holler, Jack right behind him all the way. When they got to the seep, at the head of the cove,[12] Old Tush jumped in the well-bucket and went down like a stone, the rope cutting didos[13] behind him. Now, they was under Doty Hill[14] there where the well was, and Jack just waited till the rope went slack, tied it to an oak, and clumb[15] down it. Just a-fore he hit the water, where the bucket lay afloat, he seen a side path into the ledge-rock along the side of the well. There went Old Tush, sidelong down the cave, and Jack come in a-hind him. Directly, Old Tush went around a corner, and Jack come up against a little man, setting on a stone, all dressed in motley. Beside him sat the bucket. He was a willy-waw![16]

"Howdy, Jack," said the willy-waw. "I knowed if'n I sent Old Tush up there, he'd fetch you right down!"

Jack huffed up and said, "How come d'you know my name, and how come d'you steal our supper?"[17]

"I'm sorry, Jack," said the willy-waw. "But ever'body knows about Jack, and how brave you are, and how you've had so many adventures, and all." Jack, he changed from huffing to strutting with pride, and the willy-waw went on a-praising him. "And all how you're the onliest one can help us here in the Belowground."

By now Jack was ready to fight bear with a switch, and he says, real proud-like, "I'm your man; what do you need done?"

"Well, Jack," says the willy-waw, "we got giants a-plaguing us. Three giants been a-stealing all kind of food, and taking off folks' children. Why, there's three sisters been taken off'n Doty Hill in the Belowground right now!"

"Now, I've killed me some giants a-fore," says Jack, "and it's par'lous business,[18] but I'm all for it! Tell me what to do."

"Don't never be prideful, Jack," said the willy-waw.[19] "Always take the rusty one!"

Jack didn't quite know what to make of that, but he never had no chance to ask. The willy-waw was gone in a instant; so Jack just set off down the cave-path till he come to the first giant's house. He walked up to the door of the first house; that door towered over him. Not wishing to announce his presence by a-knocking, he just pushed the door open and stepped in. There lay a pile of stolen ironwork. Jack grabbled around[20] in the heap, and sure enough, at the bottom of the pile he found a rusty broadaxe. He h'isted it up, and went a-walking through the big old house. Around the first corner, he run smack-dab[21] into a giant, twelve foot tall, packing a club and slapping his palm with it. The giant taken out after Jack, and they fit and fit[22] a terrible fight, but Jack jumped around and lopped 'at giant's head off. The giant hit the ground with a crash, and Jack heared someone a-laughing and clapping her hands, back in the shadders. Out come the purties'[23] girl he'd ever laid eyes on. Her hair was red, her skin was white, and her eyes was green. "You're purty as a speckled pup," said Jack. "Let's you and me get married, and forget about the rest of them giants!"

"Oh, no, Jack," says the girl. "We got to get my sisters free. I'm the ugly one of the bunch. They're both a whole heap purtier than me!" After a little more persuading, he follered her down the Belowground path to the next giant's house.

The second house was even bigger, and the red-haired girl hid outside whilst Jack pushed open half of the door to the place, and went in. In the great hall was another pile of stolen ironwork, taken to bedevil the Aboveground farmers, who couldn't figure out where their tools had gone. Jack dug around and pulled out a rusty old hand-scythe.

By the time he'd looked up, there was the second giant, bigger'n the first, and with two heads, both arguing over how to kill Jack, and how to cook him up after they was done killing him. Each hand had a club, and they commenced to beat on Jack something fierce. Jack, he fit back with the axe in one hand, and the scythe in t'other. It was a dreadful fight, but in time he cut off first one head, then t'other, and the giant hit the ground with a splat!

Out from behind the giant come the second sister, purtier'n the first. She had black, curly cascades of hair halfway down her back, and lips the color of wild roses. They met up with her sister, and had quite a reunion there.

"Now, girls," said Jack, "Let me marry up with one of you, and t'other can marry one of my brothers, and we can be perfectly happy, without killing that other giant."

The girls wouldn't have none of it. They talked Jack into traveling on in the Belowground, said, "Baby Sister is the purtiest of us all!"

They come to a great brake[24] of dark water, with a big stone house setting on a island in the midst of it. Jack looked at the sisters and said, "Ain't no footbridge, is there?" They both shook their heads. "There's something to keep me from swimming that brake, ain't there?" They smiled sweet-like and pointed to the cattails and cane, and he saw the biggest cottonmouth water moccasin Jack'd ever seen.

That snake was ninety foot long and had eyes as big as yeller mushmelons. Its scales was made of steel, and its tongue was like a lick of fire darting out at Jack.

Jack allowed as how he couldn't do this alone, and sent the girls to charm that snake. Holding hands and a-shaking, they went on down that hill and come up close on that snake. They went to admiring him out loud and talking on about how purty he was, and how shiny and black his scales was. The snake tucked his head down, bashful-like, and directly they went to singing silly songs for him. He was wagging his tail in time to the music, like a pup-dog, except each time he lashed that tail, the water stirred up in the brake.

Then the girls sang some old ballits,[25] and soon that snake was getting sleepy. The old ballits'll do that. He stretched out to yawn, and his head was on this bank, and his tail come clean up to the other bank. When the snake started in a-snoring Jack crossed over on his back, and went into the great stone house. Just inside the gate lay the purtiest knife he'd ever seen! That giant must've stole it from the wealthiest man Aboveground! Jack commenced to feel ashamed of these old farm tools he was a-packing, and directly he dropped them, and taken up that shiny frog-sticker. The handle was made from silver and gold, and the blade was a foot long, and honed like a razor. "Shucks," says Jack, "I might as well kill the last 'un in style." He marched on into the place, and come right up on the owner!—a giant, tall as an oak tree, with three heads, all a-laughing, and discussing what a fool Jack was. Jack swung that big knife up against the giant's two clubs, and the knife flew into gold and silver dust that sparkled up the air and drifted down on Jack. The giant raised both clubs to squarsh[26] Jack flatter'n a flitter.[27] Jack knowed right then that the knife had been witched by the giant, to fool the prideful, and he ran like a scalded possum back to the gate, before the giant's clubs fell. He heared 'em hit the ground behind him, but he grabbed up his axe and his scythe, and fit the giant to a standstill. He chopped off one head, and lopped off another, but that last head put up a powerful fight before Jack finally hacked it off, too.

Now Jack went to looking around for that third sister. She wasn't behind the giant, and she wasn't in the shadders. But he opened a little door beside the fireplace, and there she sat, in a rocking chair, so purty words couldn't describe her. Her hair was yeller like cornsilk when it first comes out in the spring; she had eyes blue like irises in the summertime. She looked at Jack and said, "Is 'e dead?"

"Yep," says Jack, "and your sisters's a-waiting."

They went back acrost the sleeping snake, and the three girls laughed and cried all at the same time when they met up with one another. Back at the well, the willy-waw had Old Tush h'ist 'em up in the bucket, and onc't Above-ground, the sisters married Jack and his brothers. Jack taken the younges', with the yeller hair. Tom married up with the black-haired girl. And Will and the sister with carrot-red hair got hitched up, too. And the brothers never again had to cook their own supper. And nobody stole it from 'em again, neither.

---

[1]Tusk or tooth (rhymes with *blush*).
[2]Omaha is in northern Boone County, Arkansas.
[3]Moving with great speed—alluding to the hub of a wagon wheel.

[4] A rock skipped across water travels quickly, with a hopping motion.

[5] There was.

[6] Swallow. It and many other words ending in *-ow* become *-er* in pure Ozark dialect. "Hard to swallow" means "hard to believe," and is a pun on the lack of food and drink.

[7] All that remained of the ham was the outer skin, or rind, darkened from smoking, usually thrown to the dogs in better households. Bread crust from a previous meal would have been saved for making dressing or for feeding to the hounds.

[8] Carrying.

[9] A cupboard with tin sheets in the doors. The tin is pierced in designs, to allow the passage of air but not of large bugs or mice. The presence of a safe in the home implies a very well-to-do hill family.

[10] Milk that has begun to "turn," or clabber.

[11] A wet-weather spring; near a natural seep is a good place to dig a well.

[12] A cove is a narrow, steep-walled valley or gully. The head is the uphill, narrower end.

[13] Scampering or cavorting. The well-rope was dancing about as it rapidly entered the well.

[14] Rotten; said of a log or fence rail. There is also a Doty family in the Omaha area.

[15] Climbed.

[16] An Ozark leprechaun; also spelled *willi-waught*. In common English, *williwaw* means a sudden gust of wind, implying capriciousness. A *williwaught* or *willy-waught* is the last dregs of a bottle of liquor drunk at a single swig. Thence the hillbilly comment, "Some says willy-waws live at the bottoms of wells; some says at the bottoms of jugs!" As for an origin for the word, it is possible that it comes from the Anglo-Saxon words *wille*, meaning (among other things) "well," and *wa*, meaning "woe" or "source of sorrow." Most creatures in a well—tantarabobuses, for example—are harmful. Willy-waws are mischievous but harmless.

[17] "How do you come to know . . .," meaning "How is it that you know . . .," is often shortened to "How come do you know . . . ."

[18] Perilous. Jack has already had some of his adventures, at least the one with the giant's bean plant, or the willy-waw would not know of his reputation.

[19] *Prideful* is used here by the willy-waw, since *proud* is often used in the Ozarks to mean *happy*.

[20] Made rooting motions—usually used to describe the motions of removing potatoes from the earth.

[21] Directly; used primarily in expressions of direction or movement.

[22] Past tense of *fight*.

[23] Phonetic for *prettiest* in Ozark pronunciation.

[24] A slough, or any place where water overflows a creek bank and stands for part of the year.

[25] Ballads.

[26] Squash—both the vegetable and the verb. This and many words ending

in *-ash* are pronounced ending in *-arsh* in the pure Ozark dialect.

[27] A fritter or pancake, taking on the punning alliteration from *flatter.*

This fascinating story was told by Informant 36, largely in fragmentary form, in the fall of 1985. He had heard it as early as 1920, but what he recounted may have been several stories put together inadvertently. Richard Chase recorded an Appalachian version under the name "Old Fire Dragaman" in *The Jack Tales* in 1943. Chase learned it from the descendants of Council Harmon, who lived from 1803 to 1896, so it could easily have traveled into the Ozarks by the 1920s. Vance Randolph calls his version "Jack and Old Tush" in *The Talking Turtle.* The elements of the rusty implements and the enchanted knife resemble the standard European hero story. The dinner bell, an iron triangle, replaces the earlier Appalachian and Ozark dinner horn, made from a cow's horn. In the Chase version, the brothers go down a sinkhole in a corf. In this Ozark version, the addition of the willy-waw provides a motivation for the stealing of the brothers' suppers, which is mysteriously unexplained in the actions of the dragaman in Chase's version.

Jack and the One-Bullet Hunt

3 **Back when Jack was still to home, and his** brothers Will and Tom had gone out to seek their fortunes, Jack decided one day to go a-hunting. They hadn't had no meat in the house for three days, and Jack, he wanted to go a-hunting!

"Your pa is away," said his ma, "and he took the rifle. But if'n you go into the back room, and you look real careful, you'll find your granddaddy's old, old shotgun. If'n you clean it up good, it'll work jus' fine. But, son, we only got the one bullet[1] for that gun."

Well, Jack figured that he was a good enough shot that one was better than none, so he cleaned that shotgun up until it just shone, put that one bullet in his pocket, hitched the mule to the wagon, and drove down, and down, and down into the holler where he was going to hunt.

Hours went by; the middle of the afternoon come, and he still hadn't found nothing to shoot with his one bullet. Well, about that time, over the hills come a flock of geese a-flying in, and they landed by the creek down in the holler. Jack thought he could snare more of them geese than he could shoot, so he snuck to the wagon and took out a fishing net. He tied up a snare out of the net and some string on some sticks, and got some corn from the bed of the wagon.

He hid, and pretty soon all four big old geese walked under the snare and commenced to eating that corn. It worked just perfect. He tripped the snare, and the net dropped on the geese, and he run out and grabbed on to the net-strings. Well, the geese took affright. They went to fighting and skonking² and flapping their wings. Pretty soon there's wings sticking out of that net in ever' direction, and them geese took flight! The geese went to flying right up in the air, and dragged Jack up behind 'em, right up in the air. He thought they'd get tired eventually and put him down. Didn't happen that way. They flew, and flew, clean to the top of the tallest oak tree in that stand of timber, and they got snagged. Jack's up there swinging from the net-strings, wondering how he's going to get down. He decided it wasn't too far to drop, if he could just get the drop perfect, and miss all the rocks and all the stumps. He got short on grip, and dropped down. He done pretty good. He missed all of the rocks and most of the stumps. He hit the top end of the tallest stump in the woods, and went feet-first into the holler of it, up to about his chest. He stuck there like the bust of Washington³ and couldn't move. At first he couldn't figure out what held him, till honey come oozing all up around him and commenced to running down the outside of the stump. That bee-tree set up a powerful suction, and he was a-squirming and a-wiggling, trying to pull his arms free and climb out. After a while, he tried to calc'late how long he could live licking up honey till his ma missed him and come a-looking for him.

Now, there's just some sounds that can't be mistook for anything else on God's green earth; bear snorts is one of 'em. Pretty soon Jack's a-hearing these bear snorts especially close on to his shoulders. When that old black bear gave Jack a swipe with his tongue, licking that honey off, Jack let out a yell and sprung halfway out of the stump. The bear gave a start and turned tail to run. Jack grabbed his free hands onto that bear's tail. The bear gave a jump and broke the stump off at the root! The bear run toward the creek, dragging Jack loose. The bear jumped clean over the creek, and Jack let go. *Splash!* Jack's in the creek.

He decided to wash all that honey off while he's there, and on the third dive, he come up choking on his collar. He felt around and found a twelve-pound catfish in his shirt, trying to get out. Jack grabbed the fish, but the weight of it snapped his collar, and Jack's collar button shot out acrost the creek and killed a pheasant dead as a doornail. Jack climbed out with the fish in one hand and took up the pheasant in t'other. He dressed 'em out, and laid 'em in the wagon, and was a-getting ready to go to the house, when in over the trees come a-gliding three wild turkeys. They roosted on the low limb of that old oak tree. Jack thought, "That's what I'll shoot with my one bullet!" So he loaded up the gun, and was creeping toward them turkeys, when that same unmistooken sound stopped him cold!

The bear's back, lured by the smell of honey, and staring at Jack reminiscent-like. Now, the bear's under the turkeys, so Jack figured he'd shoot the turkeys, and it'd scare the bear. Didn't happen that way. Jack drawed a bead[4] on them turkeys, took one more step, tripped, and spent the shell. He missed ever' single turkey, but he blowed a limb clean off the tree, and it fell and killed the bear dead as a hammer handle. The turkeys panicked. The turkeys took off and flew straight up into that net full of geese; got all tangled up in amongst 'em, and couldn't go no further. Jack looked for some way to get 'em down.

There was an axe in the wagon; you don't go nowhere in the Ozarks 'thout an axe. Now he could get all that poultry down! So, here's Jack, chopping on this old oak tree plumb up until dark. Pretty soon, that old tree creaked a couple of times, twisted around, all fell to the ground with a terrifying crash, and hit two buck deer that was standing under it. He skinned out the bear and the two buck deer by moonlight, loaded 'em in the wagon, and tossed the netful of fowl on top. That wagon's just heaped up with meat; he's proud!

But he hopped onto the seat, grabbed his reins, whopped the mule with the lines. The mule was asleep, and when Jack strapped him, he bucked and kicked, and broke the trace chains. Now Jack pondered on this, and decided to take one of them green deerskins and tie two legs to the trace chains and two legs to the single-tree. Now, this was a par'lous arrangement, and Jack knowed it, so he just led the mule to the house. He figured the deerskin ought to work good enough.

Didn't happen that way.

He come out of the holler up onto the ridge where the house was, and looked back. He was at the house, and the wagon was in the holler, and the green deerskin was stretched out between 'em like a clothesline. Jack was too tired to do anything about it tonight, so he tied the deerskin to the post oak in the yard, put the mule in the barn, and went to the loft and went to sleep. When the sun come up, the deerskin dried and shrank, and the wagon commenced to climb the hill. It hit the stump full of honey, and rolled it along in front. The whole kit and caboodle come to a stop at the post oak just as Jack come down to wash. Now, Jack's ma was right proud, but Jack, he was upset. "Ma," said Jack, "I got to go hunting again!"

"Land of Goshen," says his ma, "what for?"

"Well," says Jack, "I got a twelve-pound catfish, a pheasant, a bear, four geese, three turkeys, two buck deer and a stumpful of honey. But, Ma," he says, "I never did get to shoot nothing!"

---

[1]*Bullet* can refer to any cartridge or shell. It may in fact refer to a leather

pouch of shot that would have been loaded pouch and all, tamped down over the powder, similar to a bulla.

[2]Onomatopoeia for the squawking of geese.

[3]That is, only his shoulders, neck, and head protruded from the bee tree.

[4]Aiming off the metal bead on the end of the barrel.

This tall tale has many variants, including an Appalachian version called "Jack's Hunting Trips, Part One" in *The Jack Tales* and an Ozark version collected by Vance Randolph. Our Ozark variant is told in fragmentary form by Informant 36, and by Informant 24. Informant 7 tells it with no reference to Jack at all. This story was heard by the three informants as early as 1914, and as recently as the 1950s.

Jack and the Conjuring Woman

4 **Onc't, after Jack left home to seek his for-**
tune,[1] he'as a-walking down a country lane, and
came upon a big old house that looked deserted
and lived-in all at the same time. Laying in the
sun on the step-stone, with her paws all tucked under, was
the biggest old puss'cat he'd ever seen. Looking for something to eat, he walked up to the place, figuring to offer
some chore help in return for some vittles.[2] That old cat
looked at him real sad-like, and he reached down to pet
her, noticing she was almost red-colored, which was a
powerful odd shade for a cat to be. Just when he touched
her, she spoke up and said, "Help me, Jack!"

Jack was so startled he flew through the air and hit the
house-wall backmost-first. "What you say?" he asked.

The old puss'cat stood and said, "Help me, Jack!"

"Well," said Jack, "I come up to offer to help, in return for
something to eat, if'n you're the lady of the house!"

"An old conjuring woman[3] is the owner of this place, and
believe me, she ain't no lady."

Now, Jack had begun to figuring it out, but the puss went
on a-talking. "My name's 'Lizabeth, and she put a spell on
me. I got losted off from my family's wagons in the spring
of the year, and when I wandered up here, the old hag
witched me into staying. I can't leave the house-place, and

I couldn't-a even talked if'n you hadn't-a touched me!"

"Barn cats is easy to come by,"[4] said Jack. "Why'd she need a big old cat?"

"Silly!" said the cat, "I ain't a cat all the time! She lets me out to clean the house and do all her chores. She's a-coming back right soon, to do just that. You hide under that warshtub, there, and maybe you can he'p me."[5] About that time Jack heared the awfulest screeching and whis-tling sound coming through the trees, and the cat didn't have to tell him twic't; he throwed himself down on the porch and pulled the old barrel-tub over him. Directly he heared the old witch-woman come a-stomping up onto the porch. "Get the straw-broom and get to sweeping, child!" he heared. Then he heared a broom on the boards, sweep-ing hard, and the clomp of shoe-leather inside the house. He peeked out; there was the purtiest[6] red-haired girl he'd ever seen, a-sweeping the porch to beat sixty. He heared the old conjuring woman inside, a-singing like a busted fiddle. He took out his big old frog-sticking knife, and whispered, "I'll kill the old witch!"

"No! Not with that!" whispered 'Lizabeth. "Her hide'll turn that, sure.[7] You got to use the witch-broom, in by the fireboard![8] I can't touch it, I'm forbidden; but you can take it and beat the old witch to death! Walk in behind me!" So 'Lizabeth swep' her way into the house, stirring up a heap of dust as she went, and Jack come along behind her. The old woman was stirring the kettle, and didn't heed.[9] Jack grabbed onto the witch-broom and whupped her, and whapped her and whomped her, and down she fell. He beat on her until she come into pieces, and he swept some of the pieces into the fire. But a bunch of the pieces got away! "She ain't dead," said 'Lizabeth, "and I ain't free yet. When she comes back, she can look like anything she fancies, with her magic. But you ask me, and I'll tell you if'n it's her." Well, they're sitting in the house a-waiting, and Jack kept his broom to the ready.[10] Directly, they heared something come a-rustling through the grass and rattling over the porch-boards. The door flung open and in come this unnatural' big snake! I mean, that snake was as big around as a keg and long as a well-rope.

'Lizabeth hollered, "That's her, Jack, kill her!" Well, Jack begun to whup and whomp on that snake, and hit it so hard he knocked its head against the floor. It hissed at him, tried to wrap around his legs, and tried to pull him down, but Jack, he fit[11] with that snake and beat it to pieces. He swept the pieces into the fire, but some of the pieces got away! 'Lizabeth said, "Now, Jack, she'll be back at least twic't more!" Sure enough, directly they heared something whining and whirring off in the timber. It come a-closer and a-closer. It come to the door, and the door flung open with a bang. In come this bald-faced hornet, big as a bull-calf; had a stinger as long as your arm. "Is that her?" hollered Jack.

"That's her, Jack, kill her," hollered 'Lizabeth. Well, Jack, he went to fighting with that old hornet, and whupped her and whopped her and whomped her with that old broom, until he knocked her outen the air, and busted her into pieces on the floor. And he swept the pieces into the fire, but some of the pieces got away! Well, 'Lizabeth, she went over and built the fire until the flames was a-licking up the chimley,[12] so's none of the pieces could get away again. Directly, they heared shoe-leather stomping on the porch; the door flung open, and in come the witch. Only she was a lot littler than she had been. She weren't but two foot tall. She was a-carrying a club four foot long. Jack didn't need no help this time; it was her, all right. He commenced to fighting that old woman, but she could move like lightning. He'd make a swipe at 'er, she'd dodge; and whop him on the shins with the club. But he fit, and fit, and won the fight. He busted her into a thousand pieces, and swept 'em into the fire. That old witch sizzled and crackled and jumped for a good long while, and bits of her sparked out on the latch-rug, but now 'Lizabeth took up the broom and swept the bits back in. The witch burned all up, and the fire went cold and ever'thing turned to a fine, gray ash. 'Lizabeth, she flung her arms around Jack, and he said, "My lands! My head's a-spinning with all that's been a-going on! Are you free now?"

"Yep," said 'Lizabeth. "And you ain't had your supper yet. Set down, and let me feed you." He set right down, and she laid out a good bait of vittles.[13] While he was a-eating, she said, "Now, Jack, that old witch had a powerful stash of gold under the boards of this house, and it's yours, now that you've killed her."

"That don't hardly seem right," said Jack. "I'll half it with you!"

'Lizabeth grinned real big, and said, "Pshaw, Jack, I don't need no gold. What I need is a rich old man!" Now, it didn't take no schooling to figure that out, and Jack married up with 'Lizabeth, and they left with all that gold, and went back along the road to find her folks.

---

[1]"Seeking his fortune" does not imply seeking wealth; rather it means seeking what fate has in store for him.

[2]Victuals, or food.

[3]A conjuring woman is an herb and magic spell doctor, sometimes a good character, sometimes an evil one. In the Vance Randolph tale "Jack and the Old Witch" (in *The Talking Turtle*), the term *witch* is used throughout.

[4]To obtain.

[5]Hiding under a tub or kettle is a common trick in Jack tales, although that element is missing from the Randolph version of this tale.

[6]Prettiest.

[7]The witch's skin, or hide, is so tough it will turn the blade away harmlessly.

[8]In the Randolph version, the broom is made from mistletoe. A fire-board is a mantelpiece.

[9]Took no notice of.

[10]Holding up a weapon defensively.

[11]Fought.

[12]Chimney.

[13]*Bait*, in this sentence, has its archaic meaning—food given while in transit.

This tale seems to be a composite, with elements inserted from other Jack tales. It also violates the "rule of three," so common in folktales, in that Jack fights the witch four times. In the Randolph version, the witch is not seen in her natural form until the third bout. Informant 36 told this tale in fragmentary form, along with other fragments, and a complete Jack tale, "Jack and the One-Bullet Hunt," in the summer of 1985. He had heard them in childhood, in Omaha, Arkansas, from about 1915 to 1920.

Tall Tales

This best-known Ozark story type stretches the limits of credibility for fun.

The Meanest Man in Arkansaw

5 **There was a bunch of coon hunters sitting** out in the field, and, boy, they had it made! They was sitting there with a big old fire burning away, watching it burn. They was going to sit there and watch it burn, wait for the dogs to jump up a coon, and go to running it over the hill, so they could sit there and listen to 'em.

That's how they hunt coon in Arkansaw.

They had 'em a couple of coon carcasses on a spit roasting over the fire. Had 'em a jug, and was a-passing it around, sitting there, watching the fire burn, waiting for the dogs to start a-barking.

All of a sudden, out of the timber come the durndest noise they'd ever heared in their lives. Sounded like trees falling, branches a-snapping, and thunder rumbling! Scared 'em so bad they jumped up and went to looking for weapons.

Warn't no time! Out of the timber come the biggest man they'd ever seen afore—seven foot tall, beard plumb to his belly button, come a-riding a grizzly bear out of the timber, whupping on him with a rattlesnake.

He come a-galloping up to the fire, and whoa'd the old bear by grabbing his nose, turning his old nose aside, and just laying him down there by the fire. He walked over and

grabbed them coon carcasses, and et 'em in one swaller, bones and all. Grabbed the jug, busted the top off'n the crockery, and downed all that 'shine[1] at a swig. He dropped the jug, picked his bear up, and set it up on its feet again, jumped on its back, and said, "Fellers, I hate like ever'thing to eat and run, but the meanest son of a bitch in all of Arkansaw is right behind me."

---

[1]Moonshine.

Informant 29 told this story in 1980. He had heard it all his life, having learned it circa 1912, in or around Bay, Arkansas.

The Smartest Dog in Oklahoma

Old fella claimed he had the smartest dog in Oklahoma. Said he'd take down his deer rifle off the rack, and the dog'd bring the musk bottle from the shed. If he took down the shotgun, the dog'd start pawing the decoys out of the closet. If he pulled the sawed-off shotgun out from under the bed, the dog'd pull the chester-drawer open with his teeth and haul out the turkey calls.

Finally the fella decided to try to fool the blamed hound. He got out his fishing rod and set it on the back porch. Next thing he knew, that dog went to the trash pile, snagged a soup can, and went to digging up red worms!

Informant 33 told this one in 1988. He had heard it "forever," at least as early as 1950.

The Arkansas Rubberworm

7 **One week I was out in Beaver Lake fishing.**
I had my pole and my minnows, and was busy
wasting bait and chugging minnows going up one
side of the lake and down the other, catching
crappie—but not many. In my mind, I got to drifting, and
my boat got to drifting, and pretty soon I was over by the
bluff. I heard an awful thrashing sound over on the bluff,
and, since I wasn't having much luck fishing, I rowed over
to see what was going on.

There was a redbird there, with a worm in its beak,
trying to pull that worm out of the ground. That little bird
was flapping its wings, and huffing and puffing; it already
had two feet of worm out of the ground, but this was no
ordinary worm! I could tell right away that the hapless
bird had chanced on the rare Arkansas rubberworm. Now,
many folks are not aware that in Arkansas there are two
varieties of red worm. First there's your ordinary fishing
worm. Then there's the extremely elastic rubberworm,
very rare, and practically extinct. By now the bird was on
the ground, with its little feet dug in, its wings out and
flapping. It was backing away, stretching that worm for all
it was worth. The redbird may have been about to give up,
but by now it had attracted the attention of a red-tailed
hawk. The hawk spotted the little redbird, and folded his

wings in a dive. He swooped down on the redbird, and grasped it in his talons. In Missouri, they say the stubbornest animal is a mule, but in Arkansas the stubbornest creature is the redbird. This little bird had found that worm fair and square, and was not about to let go over a little trifle like being eaten by a hawk.

So here was this great hawk grasping the redbird, the redbird has the rubberworm in its beak, and the rubberworm has a mighty hold on the roots of the nearest oak tree. The hawk, by strength of wing, stretched that rubberworm another fifteen feet or so, him backflapping hard as he can, and the worm getting thinner and thinner. The hawk began to labor at it, making little hawkish grunts, until he reached a height of about twenty-two feet, and stalled out. Oh, he kept flapping, but he quit going anywhere. Now the worm began to fight back, and the hawk's altitude began to vary as the worm tugged first one way, then the next, with its buried end wrapped, I presumed, around the roots of that tree. Something had to give, I thought, but I wasn't prepared for what it was going to be. Deep in the bluff-face, I heard a rumble. The oak tree began to shiver as if it had a high fever. Then something snapped with a crack, then another, then another. The entire oak was yanked from the ground, and fell into Beaver Lake. At that instant the worm lost its grip on the tree roots, and the worm, the redbird, and the hawk shot into the sky headed toward Oklahoma. It was a terrible shame, too, for that may have well been the last of the rare Arkansas rubberworms.

This magnificent example of the Ozark tall tale is retold from a yarn spun by Bailey Phelps, the storytelling preacher from Rogers, Arkansas, in the summer of 1980.

The Giant Rattlesnake

O **A feller was a-driving a wagon along a** winding Ozark road, with a couple of mules hitched up to pull it, when not too far out of town, with no warning whatsoever, a giant rattlesnake sprang out of the ditch. He was as big around as a man's hat—eight foot long he was. Leaped up out of the ditch, baring fangs as long as a pocketknife blade; made a swipe at them mules. Them mules, being smart, jammed on their brakes and backed up just as far as they could in harness, and that old snake, having already taken his measure of 'em, missed both of 'em, and buried his fangs in the wagon tongue.

The old snake's fangs got hung in the wood, and he thrashed around something awful. The feller got down off the wagon and killt[1] the critter; figured the fam'ly could eat for a week on that much meat. He dug them fangs out of the tongue, and commenced to loading the thing in the wagon. He heard the biggest commotion up front; it was them mules! That old rattler had put so much venom in the tongue that it had swelled up like a pizened[2] pup, lifted them mules clean off the ground, and like to strangled 'em in their harness.[3]

The feller cut his mules down. He was a tie-hacker by trade,[4] and hitched them mules in logging harness, and

55

set one to drag home the snake, and t'other to drag that swollen wagon tongue down to the sawmill. Got it sawn up into lath, fifteen foot long; filled up a whole wagon-load of lath.

Well, he took the lath home and built him a chicken coop out of it. He went and put all his chickens in it, and then he made a fatal mistake—he painted that new chicken coop with a turpentine paint. That turpentine drawed all the pizen out of the wood;[5] and it shrunk back to its original size, and killt ever' chicken in the place.

---

[1]The past tense of verbs ending in *-l* is often pronounced with a *t;* e.g., *killt,* *spillt.*

[2]Poisoned.

[3]"Like to" is an Elizabethan hold-over for "would likely have" or "nearly."

[4]A common Ozark profession from 1890 to 1930; logs were cut and hewn with a broad axe into railroad ties.

[5]Turpentine was applied to snake bites to draw out the poison.

Informant 9 told this story in early 1979. There are many variants of it, including specific Appalachian versions, and a southwestern version about Pecos Bill. He did not remember when he had first heard it.

The Fisticuff Champeen
of Arkansaw

9 **There was this old boy who lived in Stone** County, Missouri, and, boy, he was a fighter! That boy'd rather fight as eat. He loved to pick a fight, and then fight him to a standstill, more'n anybody you ever knew. He had fit and whupped[1] ever'body from Blue Eye plumb up to Springfield and clean over to Joplin. He got right proud of hisself; got to calling hisself "The Fisticuff Champeen of Missouri."

Well, he was bragging on hisself one day, and this feller come by and heard him. And he said, "Shoot, you ain't so much! I know a feller down in Arkansaw, calls hisself 'The Fisticuff Champeen of Arkansaw.'"

Now, that got the old boy to thinking, "Doggone it, now, if I can go down there and whup up on that feller, I can be the 'Fisticuff Champeen of Missouri *and* Arkansaw.'"

So he got on his mule, and he run down to Alpena Pass, where he'd been told the feller lived. He found the cabin with no trouble, went up and banged on the door, and the feller's woman[2] come to the door. The old boy asked about him, and she said, "He ain't here right now, he's down the lane a-sowing oats."

Sure enough, the old boy rode down the lane, and here was a fine plowed field. He looked out acrost there, and way over on the other side of the field, he saw the feller a-

57

coming toward him, a-sowing oats. And he said, "Doggone it, that feller looks big!" And he could see him a-walking along there with a bed-ticking tied acrost the front of his shoulders, and he was a-sowing oats out of that bed-ticking. Not only that, but he had an A-harrow tied on to each heel and was dragging 'em along and was a-covering them oats as he sowed 'em. Well, he come up along the fence, and the old boy said, "Doggone it, he's about seven foot tall!"

The feller from Arkansaw looked down at this old boy from Missouri, and he kind of rumbled as he said, "YOU WANT SOMETHING?"

The old boy said, "No . . . no . . . no, I don't want nothing!"

The feller leaned over the fence, looked him up and down, and said, "YOU SURE YOU DON'T WANT SOME-THING?"

The old boy kind of gritted his teeth, and said, "Are you . . . the fisticuff champeen . . . of Arkansaw?"

The feller growled, "YEAH! I AM! WHAT'S IT TO YOU?"

The old boy gulped and said, "Well, you're the champeen of Missouri, now, too!"

---

[1]Fought and whipped.

[2]*Woman* always meant *wife* in the Ozarks, including common-law wife.

Informant 17 told this story in the summer of 1981. His father told him the story in Stone County in about 1949.

Old Ned

10 **I had a horse named Ned, when I** was younger; that Ned was so smart he'd come when you held up the bridle. He'd grab the bit like it was a stick of peppermint candy, and flip the straps over his ears. If I'd hang the saddle off the right branch of the blackjack tree, old Ned'd walk under and saddle himself. Best yet, he'd always do what I told him. We was out a-riding onc't, when along come the Baldknobbers[1] a-chasing us. They was firing off their guns and hollering something awful, so we didn't stick around to find out what they wanted; we rode hard up the nearest hill. Me and old Ned came to a high bluff, unexpected, and had nowheres to go. Fifty Baldknobbers right behind us! It was two hundred foot down, but it was the only way out. "Giddy-up, Ned," I hollered, and we went over the edge of the bluff. We fell a hundred and ninety-seven foot. "Whoa, Ned," I hollered, and old Ned stopped. Then I said, "C'mon, Ned, a three-foot fall never killed nobody!"

We was halfway home when a pack of grizzly bears rared up out of the timber. There was no way out. Them bears et old Ned, best horse I ever had. But I got even. When ever' one of them bears had a big mouthful, I just hollered, "Whoa, Ned." Ned whoa'ed, and ever' bear choked to death.

[1]The Baldknobbers were a post–Civil War gang of vigilantes, a protection organization that turned to crime by the first part of this century.

Informant 25 told this story in the summer of 1980. He had heard it in the general store in Elkland in about 1950.

The R'arin'-Up, Tearin'-Up Scoonkin Hunt

11 **The old man never could talk** straight, 'cep' when he was drunken, and we'uns's[1] powerful poor, what with his inheritance and all, so he allowed as how he'd take the old woman off the mantel and kiss his shotgun goodbye, and we'uns'd[2] go to hunting some scoonkins to sell at the stain tration when the next caboose came by alone.[3] He went out to whistle up all the hounds, all 'cep' Old Shorty. Now, Shorty, he was a purebred, half shepherd and half dash-hound, fast as molasses and mean as milk. Then he whistled up Old Shorty. Me, I went out to the horse to saddle up my barn and try to catch up to Pa, who hadn't left yet. I led the old tree stump up aside Old Lightning. Nobody called him that 'cep' me, and I didn't call him that, either. Then I stepped on the horse, jumped onto the stump facing back'ards, and yelled, "Let's go home, Lightning!"

Well, we lit out of there at a dead walk.[4] Pa had all the dogs rounded up, 'cep' Old Shorty. Then he rounded up Old Shorty.

We rode down a long, straight path that wound all around in the woods, till we come to a clearing full of trees with one little cabin sitting all by itself in among twelve others just like it. I climbed down off'n my tree stump and left it to graze, and walked up and beat on the woman, and a door answered.

I took off my head, and bowed my hat, and asked in a brazen, humble sort of way, if'n she'd seen my pa. "Big feller?" she says. "Yep," says I. "On horseback?" she says. "Yep," says I. "With a pack of dogs?" she says. "Yep," says I. "Ain't seen him!" she hollered in a whisper, and slammed the door in my face and invited me in. "There's nothing to eat in the house 'cep' for flapjacks and cornbread and beans and ham, but you're welcome to stay as long as you leave."

I stayed a while, and then her bark came up and started dogging at me, and I remembered Pa and all the hounds. All 'cep' Old Shorty. Then I remembered Old Shorty.

I rode hard and fast to catch up with Pa, but my tree stump tripped on somebody's horse, and throwed me face down, flat on my back, and tore my hide and bruised my shirt. So I went to see my sweetheart Sally so she'd patch my hide with a thimble and thread.

She was so glad to see me that she had the door nailed shut, so I went on in and throwed my hat on the fire and stirred up the bed.[5] We sat down right close together, her in one corner and me in the other. We commenced to playing at cards, and she drawed a heart and I drawed a diamond, and her pa come home and drawed a club.

I rode hard and fast to catch up with Pa, and passed hun'rds of coons running around 'thout their skins, so I knowed Pa'd been there. Now, all the dogs's trailing, all 'cep' Old Shorty. Then Old Shorty commenced to trailing, too. Then directly all the dogs treed, all 'cep' Old Shorty. Then Old Shorty treed, too.

Well, I jumped off my tree stump, and it ran away and sold my saddle to a city feller. So I stepped on the dogs, and commenced to climbing that syc-eye buckamore tree where them dogs'd treed two full-grown baby possums. I climbed out on a sturdy dogwood limb, and the possums started throwing acorns at me. So I climbed in a knothole and fell through the tree. I landed on all them dogs, 'cep' for Old Shorty. Then I landed on him, too.

Them possums started laughing so hard, they fell out of that tree, and I beat their heads against mine and killed 'em, and cut off their tails up close behind the ears.

When we'uns got to house, we didn't have nothing but two possum tails, a hun'rd scoonkins, a bruised shirt, no hat, no saddle, and all the dogs.

'Cep' for Old Shorty. Him and the stump never did come home.

---

[1] *We'uns,* or *we-ones,* is a standard Ozark colloquialism created by regularization from the need for a plural of "you." You in the singular is "you," and in the plural is "you-ones" or *you'ns.* From that, natives extrapolated the redundant *we-ones, we'uns,* or *we'ns. We'uns's* is, of course, the contraction for *we-ones was.*

[2] We-ones would.

[3] The caboose coming by alone is both a joke and a separate folktale: around Harrison, there are tales of a phantom caboose on the Missouri and North Arkansas Line that moved silently along the tracks at night, back in the 1920s.

[4] "Light a shuck" is an Ozark phrase meaning to leave in haste, and the expression "lit out" is its past tense.

[5] Throwing the hat on the bed is a sign of intimacy. Ozarkers are divided on the outcome of placing a hat on a bed; in the deep woods, it's a sure bringer of bad luck. In some other places the bed, usually in the same single room as most of the other furniture, is the rightful place for a large group of guests to lay their hats and coats. For a single man to lay his hat on a sweetheart's bed has sexual overtones. In fact, this entire narrative is an extended dirty joke implying intimacy between the narrator and the two women he visits.

This narrative is an Ozark version of an Appalachian tale and custom. Richard Chase in *Grandfather Tales* identifies it as the drunken or comic doctor's speech in a Christmas presentation called the English Mummers' Play. He acknowledges there are many versions, and the editors of this collection have heard numerous versions and fragments from many different informants. To our knowledge, however, this is the first version in print which explains the title as a spoonerism for *coonskin.* This version is principally from fragments told by Informants 1 and 23. They heard parts of it as early as 1935, but it is much older.

Cloverine Salve

12 **Of all the sov'reign[1] remedies, pat**ent medicines, and nostrums be-known to man, there was one that we valued above the rest, and that was Cloverine Salve.[2] The active ingredient is turpentine oil, and Granny, she put a lot of store in turpentine. Not a thing could go wrong with your exteriors that couldn't be healed right up, or at least be made to smell better, with an application of Cloverine Salve. We had this little beagle dog by name of Tige, and how he loved to run them rabbits! Well, one day, Daddy was a-running the sawmill, rough-cutting some lumber, and old Tige jumped a rabbit off in the timber. He yipped all acrost the field, through the high grass, the yips coming closer and getting more frequent as he got closer to the rabbit and closer to us. Out of the grass shot this-here rabbit, with Tige right on his tail, yipping up a storm. The rabbit cut to the left, and Tige was right behind him; he cut to the right, and Tige was with him all the way. The rabbit come into the shed, and like he'd planned it, he hit a sharp left at the sawblade. Tige flew into the shed, seen the rabbit a-turning, scrabbled his paws in the dirt to make the turn, and ran full-tilt, nose-first into that buzz saw!

It sundered him half in two, clean as a whistle![3] Quick-like, we grabbed the tin of Cloverine Salve, and slathered[4] the halves with it, slapped the two halves together, rolled Tige up in a rag, and put him in the corner behind the wood stove. That salve done the trick, all right. We'd put a bowl of milk back there, and Tige'd lap it up from his rag-bandage. In two days, the rag-bandage was sitting up, taking nourishment. But on the day after that, Tige crawled out of the rag bundle and we realized we'd bobbled it up.[5] In our haste to get Tige back together, we'd got him front-ways-back'ards-end-to-end. Two feet did touch the ground, but t'other two stuck up in the air. He'd healed up fine, although it was hard to tell if he was coming or leaving.

Old Tige got to be even a better rabbit hunting dog than before. First, he could see rabbits in either direction; none got by him. And when he went to chasing one, he'd run till one set of legs got tired, then he'd flip over and run on t'other set a while. And downhill—why he'd just end-over-end[6] the whole way down. Not a rabbit in the county could get away, downhill. And we had the only dog in the county that could bark out of both ends.

---

[1]The acknowledged best.

[2]Cloverine Salve is a registered trademark, manufactured by Medtech Laboratories, Inc., Cody, Wyoming.

[3]Very neatly, with no ragged edges, for example.

[4]Spread liberally, as with butter.

[5]Erred.

[6]Somersault.

Informant 1 told a version of this tale since the 1930s. Informant 34 told it in this form in 1979, having heard it as early as the late 1920s in Missouri.

One Bullet Left

13 **I went a-hunting yesterd'y, and was** a-feared I'd come home emptyhanded. My pa always said, if you can't shoot enough to eat with just three bullets, you deserve to go hungry! And here I'd shot and missed twic't. Only had the one bullet left. Just then I heared something in the underbrush ahead to my left. It was a buck deer! I was about to draw down on him, when I seen a big, black bear in the brush to my right. I looked at the deer, and I looked at the bear, and it didn't seem right to leave either one behind, so, quick, I drawed out my knife. I threw my knife into the elum[1] tree right a-twixt 'em, and fired at it. The knife-blade peeled that bullet right in half, and the one half of it killed the deer, and t'other half killed the bear! The jolt of the bullet knocked the hunting knife up into the midst of a flock of ducks flying overhead. It was spinning so hard it killed, cleaned, and dressed seven ducks a-fore it landed point-first on a rabbit and killed it. I was so excited, I ran over to look at the deer, and tripped over a turtle, and fell in the crick. When I tried to get back out, to catch the turtle who was lying on his back, I could hardly move, my boots was so full of bass. I bagged it all up in the bearskin, and carried it home. It was a tolerable good day's hunting for having only one bullet left.

[1]Elm.

Informant 36 told this tall one in its entirety in the autumn of 1987. He told it in response to a discussion of the Ozark Jack tale "Jack and the One-Bullet Hunt," for which he provided fragments of the version in this collection. He had heard this version in about 1920, told as the truth, of course.

The Fish in the Millpond

14 **There was a mill built along a** stream, among the hills, and the stream had been dammed to make a millpond. Out from the pond was a millrace[1] that undershot the wheel[2] when there was grinding to be done. It just happened that one lonely fish got trapped in the millpond and couldn't get over the spillway to go downstream. As time went on, the grain that drifted and sifted outa the mill fell in the water, and the fish ate it. Chil'en threw grain out to him from time to time, and he commence to grow. He et up all the littler fish, then he et the middling fish,[3] and he et the big fish. Directly, he was picking off cattle up along the stream-bank. It got to where there was more fish in the pond than water. The miller decided he was going to have to kill that fish! He tried seining him with a chicken coop, but he got away. He tried hooking him with a logging chain, but he broke off the hook. He directly tried a cannon from the War Between the States.

He missed him on the first volley, but that old fish seen him reloading, and backed upstream as hard and fast as he could back-fin.[4] He backed up so fast all the water in the millpond raced upstream with him. The water in the millrace backed up next, and finally, the water down in

68

the spillage got to running upstream, turned the under-shot wheel back'ards, and unground two bushels of corn!

---

[1]Narrow canal that carries water to the millwheel.

[2]An undershot millwheel is turned by water running under it.

[3]For some Ozarkers, *middling* is an impolite word, implying the genitals (in the middle of the body). For others it offers no offense whatsoever. Compare Vance Randolph's comments on middlings to R.E. Thomas's *Popular Folk Dictionary of Ozarks Talk* (Little Rock: Dox Books, 1971).

[4]Back-fin means, presumably, to show fins above the water while doing a backstroke.

The tale appears to be only a fragment of a longer one. It was swapped to the editors in 1986 by an unidentified informant, who called it "an old 'un."

The Best Bait Around

15 **There was this old boy who could** always catch more catfish 'n anybody. Nobody could outdo him with any snag, lure, or bait. Not even dynamite could beat him.[1] The boys down at the feed store 'llowed as how they'd lay out alongside the brush at the lake the next time he went out, and fetch his secret. Sure enough, he came along in a boat purt soon,[2] sowing chaws off'n a tobacco plug.[3] When he came in to the bank to wait a minute, the boys just couldn't stand it anymore. They was dying of curiosity. One of 'em jumped up and confronted him. "What good does tobacco do?" he demanded.

"Well," confessed the fisherman, "I leave off good chaws of the best tobacco, and the catfish come up and take it to chew. When they come back up to spit, I club 'em with a baseball bat."

---

[1]Dropping dynamite into a lake to stun or kill the fish is a dangerous and illegal method used in south Arkansas and north Louisiana to obtain large quantities of fish in a very short time.

[2]Fairly soon.

[3]Throwing small cuts off a plug of chewing tobacco.

Informant 22 told this tall tale in the summer of 1975. His father told it to him in about 1966.

How Rabbit Fooled Fox

16 **Fox was hungry! He was a-trotting** along with his sides all caved in, his ribs a-showing bad, trotting along looking for something to eat. He came up to Rabbit's house, and there sat Rabbit. "Oh, boy," thought Fox, "I'll just eat Rabbit!" So he ran up to Rabbit and said, "Rabbit, I'm a-going to have to eat you!"

"Oh . . . " allowed Rabbit, "that'll be all right. You caught me fair and square. But ain't it a shame that I didn't get to tell anybody the secret of my success!" Well, Fox got to looking at Rabbit, and sure enough, Rabbit did look awful prosperous. He had on a brand-new velvet vest, had a little gold watch-chain that run over and attached onto his watch. Setting there on his front porch, with his big old feet kicked back, puffing on his pipe!

"Aw," said Fox, "you do look awful prosperous, Rabbit. How did you get that way?"

"Well, Fox," said Rabbit, "since you done asked, I'll tell you. What you do is go out in the world, and when them human critters come by in one of their buggies, you chase them buggies, and you chase 'em, and chase 'em! When you chase 'em fast enough, the back wheels'll catch up to the front wheels, and the whole thing'll fall over, and just spill all their gold out onto the road!"

"Really?" said Fox.

"Yeah," said Rabbit, "and there goes one right now!"

Sure enough, Fox looked up, and there went one of them human critters went by in a buggy, cutting up sixty! Fox took out a-running, and he chased that there buggy, and he chased it, and he chased it. He ran till his tongue hung out onto the road, and the back wheels never caught up to the front 'uns, the contraption didn't fall head-over-wheels, and not a speck of gold fell out. Fox plopped down exhausted, at the edge of the road, panted for a few minutes; thought about it, and said to himself, "Well, I must not be doing it right. Either that or you shouldn't oughta chase a westbound 'un. Here comes another 'un now." And another buggy swooped by, and he chased that buggy, and he chased it, and he chased it. Directly he dropped into the grass, and said to himself, "I ain't making any headway! I bet that Rabbit lied to me!" He ran back over to Rabbit's house and said, "Rabbit! You made that up, didn't you? You didn't chase no buggies to get this prosperous! You lied to me!"

"Shoot," said Rabbit, "I didn't think it'd work, but 'at other fox said that you'd believe it."

Fox went all squint-eyed. "What other fox?" he asked.

"Well," said Rabbit, "the one down the well, that told me that you was so foolish that you'd believe any cockamamy lie I wanted to tell you."

What other fox? said Fox, getting his dander up.

"That old fox that lives down my well," said Rabbit.

Well, Fox ran over and peered down the well. Sure enough, way down in the well, in a little bright spot, he could see another fox looking at him.

"WHAT-A YOU BEEN TELLING THEM LIES FOR?" yelped Fox.

And the fox down the well said, ". . . You . . . been . . . telling . . . them . . . lies . . . lies . . . lies . . ."

Then Fox hollered down, "YOU BETTER QUIT THAT, OR

I'M A-GOING TO WHUP YOU!"

And the fox down the well said, ". . . I'm . . . a-goin' to . . . to . . . whup . . . you . . . you . . . you . . ."

Now Fox was so mad, 'cause foxes can't abide being around other foxes, and he hollered, "I'M A-GOING TO KILL YOUUUU!"

And the fox down the well said, ". . . Kill . . . youuuu . . . youuuu . . . youuuu . . ." Fox just jumped down that well to do battle with that fox down the well. When he heared the splash from the well, Rabbit got up from his porch-rail, knocked his pipe clean, and hopped over to put the lid on his well. He sent out word for his kith and kin to come and dig a new well the next day, and he never concerned himself with what foxes did or didn't chase ever after.

This Ozark tale, in the style of Br'er Rabbit, also contains a hint of South-eastern Indian lore—the rabbit is associated in Algonkian/Cherokee tales with tricking and well-digging. Informant 40 spun this yarn in 1988, having heard it from her mother twenty-five years earlier.

The Toler'ble Muddy Day

17 **One year it come the biggest rainy** year anybody'd ever seen. All the cricks flooded, and liked to[1] drownded us, and all the bottomland went all gumbo. Nevertheless, I had to go to the post office that day, and it wasn't but half-a-quarter[2] to the place, so I figured I'd walk. Got my big old walking staff, just to get along, but the further I'd walk the bigger my boots'd get. The walking stick was to scrape my boots off!

Then I looked up and seen something coming along the road toward me. It looked like a critter, little critter, kinda swimming along in the mud toward me. It was the wrong color for a coon, and the wrong shape for a possum. Poor little critter was so mired down, I couldn't see no little old legs.

The thing come right up to me, and I seen it was a man's hat. I picked it up, and there was a feller's head in the mud underneath of it! He looked up and said, "Howdy-do. Nice day, ain't it?"

I looked down at him and said, "Ain't it toler'ble[3] muddy to go a-walking?"

"Naw," said the feller, "I ain't a-walking. I'm riding a mule."

[1]Almost.

[2]Half-a-quarter would be half the distance along the side of a quarter-section (160 acres) of land, or one-quarter mile.

[3]Substantially.

This tall tale was told is a slightly different form by Informant 33, and a more Ozark fragment has been told by Informant 22. This particular wording was brought here by a native Louisianian in 1983, although an Oklahoma joke version was heard by the editors as long ago as 1960.

The Whoofenpoof

18 **Late at night, 'round our place, the** hounds'd go to barking for no reason, and I'd say to Grandma, "What's out there, Granny?"

And Granny'd smile, and rock, and said, "Don't fret none, child, it's just the whoofenpoof."

And all the chil'en'd gather around Granny and she'd go to telling about the whoofenpoof.

"That there whoofenpoof is a critter that runs up and down the hills at night chasing its shadow in the dark. It runs so fast, the hounds can't catch it or even see it. That's why you've never seen one.

"And it runs back'ards, a-picking its tracks up behind it as it goes, so that's why you never find its tracks.

"So if'n the hounds bay at night, and you go out to look, and you can't see nothing—and you go out the next morning, and you can't find no tracks—well, you're sure certain that the whoofenpoof's been there!"

Informant 27 told this fragment in 1984. She heard it from her grandmother in about 1978.

A-Crossin' the White

19 **Seventy years ago,**[1] **a family from** Fort Smith used to run cattle drives from there, across the Ozarks, up to the eastern railhead at Springfield, Missouri. To get from home to Springfield, they had to cross the south fork of the White River,[2] and it was deep and swift and cold.

One wet year, they drove the herd through, and couldn't get the cattle to swim the river nohow.[3] They tried and they tried to run the cattle into the current, but they just wouldn't go.

What they done was, they found this big old holler[4] tree at the side of the river, and took out axes and felled it acrost the White. It was holler clean through, and so big around that they just drove the cattle straight through the middle of it to the other side.

Drove ninety head through, and when they come out the other side, they was missing fifteen head. They rode back in to look, and sure enough, there was ten head inside, a-wandering around lost, and five of 'em had got out through a knothole!

---

[1]This would have put the alleged event in 1919.

[2]The White River in Arkansas.

[3]By no means.

[4]Hollow; many other words are pronounced thus, including *follow (foller)*, *swallow (swaller)*, and *wallow (waller)*.

Informant 20 told this tall tale in 1982. He said it "happened to his daddy" in the 1920s. He smiled when he said that, of course.

The Thousand-Legged Worm

2O **In a little old cabin at the edge of** the woods lived a little old woman, her little old man, a little girl, a little boy, and his pet fox squirrel named Chitter that he'd raised up from a kit. That squirrel'd sit right up at table and eat with the family, mostly hickory nuts, but he especially loved them light-bread[1] biscuits. Now, one day that old woman set out to bake some biscuits; took out some flour, took out some grease, and she looked in her can of saleratus,[2] and she said, "Doggone it! I can't bake no biscuits—I am clean out of sally-rat-us powder."

So she looked at her boy and said, "Take this here nickel, and get on down to the store and fetch me a can of sally-rat-us."

The boy skipped on down toward the store at the crossing and stopped at the footbridge to play with the thousand-legged worms that come out in summer and crawl amongst the leaf-rot. He didn't see them two red eyes a-staring at him out from under the bridge. He skipped on down to the store, and fetched the can of saleratus, and come a-skipping back.

Well, he was a-singing out loud, "Sally-rat-us, Sally-rat-us, Sally-rat-us."

He stirred up the booger-bear that denned up under the

79

old log bridge.³ That there booger-bear come out a-spitting damnation and snorting fire.⁴

"You . . . with the sally-rat-us . . . I'm a-going to eat you up, and your sally-rat-us, too!" And he grabbed the little boy and his can of saleratus, and he swallered him right down, whole.

Directly, the old woman was waiting at the house, and when her boy didn't come home, she sent her little girl out to look for him. Well, here went the little girl, a-sashaying down to the store. The man at the store told her, "He's done been here and gone. You better go look for him."

So she sashayed back acrost the footbridge, and sat down on the logs for a spell, and dangled her feet off the edge, kicking on the beams. Up stirred the booger-bear, and out he come.

"I et up the sally-rat-us, and I et up the little boy! And I'm a-going 'o eat you up, too!" And he grabbed the little girl, and swallered her, pigtails and all.

Well, directly, the old woman was waiting at the house, and when her little boy and little girl don't show up, she sent her old man out to hustle them kids along.

The old man tromped on down to the store, and the storekeeper said, "Them kids must be playing alongside the trail somewheres. You better go look for 'em."

The old man come a-stomping back acrost the bridge, madder'n fire at his kids, and the noise stirred up the booger-bear.

"I et up the sally-rat-us, I et up the little boy, I et up the little girl! And I'm a-going 'o eat you up, too!" And he took the old man and swallered him right down.

Directly, the sun was about to go down, and ain't nobody come home yet! So the old woman said to the pet squirrel: "I don't believe they're a-coming home. I'm a-going to look for 'em myself. If'n I ain't home by sundown, get down the gun and come a-looking."

The squirrel looked at the long-rifle over the fireplace

80

mantel, and just shook his head. The old woman hobbled on down the trail to the store. The storekeeper told her, "Now, all them folks can't be playing alongside the trail! You better go look for 'em yourself."

Back went the old woman, a-calling out their names, and she hollered as she crossed the footbridge, and stirred up the booger-bear. Out he crawled, but it was getting to be a tight squeeze under there.

"I et up the sally-rat-us, and I et up the little boy, and I et up the little girl, and I et up the old man, and I'm a-going 'o eat you up, too!" And he swallered up the old woman, cane and all.

Dark come, and the pet squirrel set out to find his fam'ly, but without the rifle-gun, as 'twere. He ran acrost the footbridge, and all the thousand-legged worms was crawling around at dusk. The squirrel stopped on the bridge, follering the scent like a itty-bitty[5] hound dog. He r'ared up and chittered out loud, to see if'n anyone'd answer.

Out come the booger-bear, huffing and puffing, plumb full.

"I et up the sally-rat-us, and I et up the little boy, and I et up the little girl, and I et up the old man, and I et up the old woman, and . . . if'n I can . . . I'm a-going to eat you up, too!"

But just as he grabbed at the squirrel-pup, that foxy critter grabbed up a itty-bitty pawful of them thousand-legged worms, and dropped 'em in the booger-bear's big old maw.

Now, them little worms wiggled, and wriggled, and tickled[6] the booger-bear's gullet, and he whooped, and

laughed, and rolled all around on the logs, and fell into the gap.[7]

The old booger-bear busted wide open, and out come the can of saleratus, out come the little boy, out sashayed the little girl, out tromped the old man, madder'n fire, and out come the little old woman . . . and her cane.

And she picked up the saleratus in one hand and that pet squirrel Chitter in t'other, and they lit a shuck for home.[8]

The old woman made the finest panful of light-bread biscuits they'd ever et. And that squirrel, he et like a king. He et the little boy's biscuit, he et the little girl's biscuit, he et the old man's biscuit, he et the old woman's biscuit, and if'n you don't watch out, he'll eat your biscuit, too!

---

[1]Made from wheat flour rather than corn meal.

[2]Sal aeratus, a leavening powder.

[3]In addition to the ordinary wild animals of the Ozarks, there are said to be booger animals, which are supernatural versions of the natural creatures.

[4]Boogers, Baptist preachers, and certain politicians possess the ability to snort damnation and spit fire.

[5]Corruption of *little-bitty.*

[6]The booger-bear suffers the internal problems of "The Old Woman Who Swallowed a Fly." This is an example of diffusion or migration of motifs.

[7]A narrow gully.

[8]Hurried.

This story has many variants, including the Appalachian version "Sody Sallyraytus" in *The Grandfather Tales* by Richard Chase. The Ozark version came in fragments from Informants 24 and 13. Informant 13 said he had heard it from his grandmother as early as 1949. He provided the editors with the fragments in the fall of 1987.

The Hoop Snake

2 1 **Out on the grass prairie, at the end** of the hills, there wasn't enough trees to make a house, just buck-bushes. Grandma pined and pined for a real lumber house, but sod had to do. One day, at the foot of a little hill, Grandpa was working, when he heard the whirling sound of the dreaded hoop snake.

Now, a hoop snake is black, and marked like a rattler and a cottonmouth crossed; it has a stinger on the end of its tail. It slithers up hills, but onc't on top, it whips itself up into a loop, bites onto its own tail, and rolls like a wheel-tire[1] down on its prey.

Grandpa had gotten in a snake's territory, and it was defending its honor. Grandpa ran around and about, with the snake rolling along behind. He ducked and he dodged, and at last, dashed behind a buck-bush. The snake rolled straight for Grandpa, and when the old feller jumped behind the bush, the snake misjudged the shot, and straightening out like an arrow, it drove its stinger into the trunk of that bush.

Grandpa came out like a shot, and killed the snake with his sod knife.

When he went back by that bush the next day, it had swollen into the hugest buck-tree you could imagine, all from that hoop snake's venom. Knowing how much Grandma wanted a lumber house, Grandpa cut down the buck-tree and ripsawed it into boards. He put up a fine board house, and they moved all their house-plunder[2] in.

Things went along fine for a day or two, but soon the venom wore off, and the house began to shrink.

By noon it was a cottage.

By sundown it was a shed.

By morning they had the best-furnished birdhouse in Oklahoma.

---

[1]The iron rim on the outside of a wooden wagon wheel is called a tire.
[2]Household belongings.

This tall tale was told by Informant 16 in 1986. He had heard it from his grandfather forty years before. For a similar story, see "The Giant Rattle-snake," story number 8 in this collection.

The Partic'lar Smart Coon

22 **Once this feller claimed to have a** coon dog that never missed a tree. Said if that dog run to a tree and barked, there was a coon up 'ere.

And he said that went on for years, then all of a sudden the dog, he went to missing!

And he got to worrying about him, saying, "Doggone, what's a-matter with m'dog?"

Then he found out it wasn't the dog, it was the coon! He'd come up against a partic'lar smart coon! Whensomever something got after that coon, he'd run down in this holler, where the fog is always partic'lar thick of a night, and he'd climb this partic'lar tree.

Whilst the dog was a-barking up that one, that old coon'd run acrost the fog to another tree, and climb down, and get away!

Informant 24 told this in the spring of 1980. He did not indicate when he had heard it.

Ring That Bell

23 **There was a pioneering family** packing the wagon to move to Missouri, and the old man brought a great big wooden crate and loaded it on. The old woman wanted to know what it was, but he just said, "Never you mind; you'll see when we get there."

They wagon-trained acrost into the Ozarks and struck off into the hills. After they'd built the cabin and got the barn up, the old man unpacked what was in the crate: it was a fine brass bell, and he hung it in its lyre on a post outside the yard.

"Now, when I'm outen the house," he said to the old woman, "and a emergency comes up, you ring this-here bell. But just for a emergency! You ring that bell, and I'll come a-running!"

A few days later, he was two solid miles away, tie-hacking,[1] and he heared the bell. He rode the mule hard up the hill and down the gully, and got to the house, and said, "What's the matter?"

And she said, "The spring-pipe's busted!"[2]

"That ain't no emergency!" the old man hollered, and he fixed up the pipes and went back to the cabin. "Ring that there bell just in a emergency! You ring that bell, and I'll come a-running!"

A week later on, he was four miles down the lane, and he heared that bell a-ringing. He jumped on that mule, whupped it hard, and rode down the lane, through the holler, over the bluff road, and down the trail till he come to the cabin. He slid to a stop and ran into the house.

The old woman said, "I can't get these childr'n to mind me!"

He went to whupping on the childr'n, and hollered, "A emergency! Just for a emergency! I can whup the kids any time! If there's a e-mer-gen-cy, you ring that bell and I'll come running!"

Two weeks later, on a blustry day, he was seven solid miles acrost the creek, and he heared that bell a-ringing. He jumped onto the mule, and rode through briars and blackberry canes, over the mud wash, acrost the rock ledge, down in the cove, and up over the ridge, till the mule c'llapsed from exhaustion. He ran two miles through the wind and another mile through the rain, and stole a horse at the crossroads store; rode through lightning and hail and sleet and snow, with branches breaking behind him, over a fallen tree and into the yard.

The cabin was gone, the barn was flat as a flour sack, and the chimley was a pile of rocks. All the trees was down, and all the livestock gone. The brass bell was lying on its lyre in the dirt, and the old woman and the childr'n was peering outen the root cellar, where the door'd been.

Off over the next hill, a big black twister wind was carrying off his good long-handles from the warshline.

"Well," the old man said, "now that's more like it!"

---

[1]Tie-hacking—cutting ties for the railroad—was a common Ozark profession.

[2]A spring-pipe brings water from a seep or spring above the level of the cabin, downhill to the dwelling.

Vance Randolph recorded a similar tale about a woman and a windstorm, but this version came from Informant 12 and several other informants who gave fragments. This story came to the editors first in 1984, from the principal informant who had heard it "all his life."

The Dogs' Tale

24 **You know how them tiny little** young'uns'll come up to you, ankle-biter-size childr'n;[1] they'll come up to you and just smile, and then, in that voice that'll pierce steel, they'll ask the most embarrassing questions you can possibly imagine . . . and they save 'em up till your house is a-full of comp'ny. Us bigger kids, we knowed Granddaddy consider'd 'em kid questions to be a challenge, and we'd sweet-talk those little kids, and bribe 'em—teach 'em the mos' unmentionable questions we could think up, and send 'em to Granddaddy. We knowed Granddaddy, if he didn't know the answer, wasn't going to say he didn't know! He was going to lie!

So one day, we sent this young'un up to say: "Granddaddy, how come is it, when you see 'em two strange dogs meeting each other for the first time, the first thing they do is run over and go to sniffing on each other's tails?"

And Granddaddy said, "Darling, there's a reason for that!

"Years ago, all of the dogs on Sunday morning'd go to the dog church. They'd go trooping into the dog church, and when they come in the back door—you know how men, when they go to church, they'll take their hats off and hang 'em on a hat rack at the back of the church—well, the dogs'd come in, and to be polite, they'd take their tails off,

89

and hang 'em on the tail-end rack at the back of the dog church.

"They'd go in, sit on the pews, howl hymns, and listen to the dog-preaching.

"One Sunday morning during the preaching, the church caught on fire! The preacher spotted the flames, and barked, 'Fire! Fire! All you dogs . . . . Git!'

"Ever'body jumped up and run out the back door, and as they passed the tail-end rack, they just grabbed a tail and went on. Darling, not one of them dogs got his rightful tail.

"And to this very day, that's what them dogs is a-doing, they're still a-looking for their very own tails!"

---

[1]Children who have just begun to walk and talk.

Informant 31 recounted this tale in the fall of 1981. The young woman heard it from her grandfather in the early 1950s. Several other versions exist, including one obscene one and one that has the dogs playing poker at the time of the fire, but this version is the finest.

Lies

Lying is a storytelling art in the Ozarks. These stories are short and "tall" at the same time.

The Cold-Trailing Coon Dog

25 **There was a fellow who kept brag-**
ging and bragging about his wonderful
cold-trailing coon dog, who could follow
any trail, no matter how old. He kept
bragging about what a fine nose this old dog had, and what
a cold trail he could follow. Finally the boys he worked
with got tired of listening to him, and said, "We want to see
just how good this dog of yours really is!"

"Sure," said the fellow. "You-all come on over to my place
tomorrow, and we'll run him."

Well, the next day they took that old hound dog out into
the woods and sicced him on the trail, and he ran around
in a circle till he picked up a scent. He sniffled and he
snuffled, and then off he went, baying and barking.

The boys took up the chase, over hill and dale, down the
gullies, across the ditches, running right along behind this
dog. The hound was leaping through the grass, baying at
every jump. About a half-a-mile from where they started,
he was running across this big, open, empty, flat field.

Barking real excited, like he was about to tree, this dog
ran straight across the field; right in the middle of the field
he stopped, jumped straight up in the air, came right back
down, and ran on toward the trees.

Right at the edge of the field, he skittered to a stop and
barked "treed."

Well, that bunch of boys ran over and caught up, and looked in the dry gulch where the dog was barking. There was nothing left of that raccoon this dog had been chasing except a skeleton. The bones were dry and white and turning to dust.

"Doggone," said the old boys from work. "We've never seen a dog that could follow a trail that cold!"

One of them said, "The only thing I don't understand is, why did that dog run across there and jump right straight up in the middle of this field?"

The fellow that owned the dog scratched his chin and said, "Well . . . there used to be a fence there."

Informant 15 told this Oklahoma version of a Texas story in 1981. He had heard it in the 1950s.

One-Eyed Jack

26 **Onc't a rich widder-woman¹ lived** all alone in a cabin high up on a ridge. She was so rich; and she kept all her cash-money with her in the cabin all the time. But it wasn't in a sock in her mattress, it wasn't in a jar buried in the yard, and it wasn't stashed in the hearth-rock. She kept it in a gallon Mason jar stuffed full of cash-money, right smack up on the fireplace mantel in plain sight. She'd use part of it to light the fire now and again. This woman was rich!

But she'd lived by herself for so long, she'd latched onto a great many peculiar ways. Like, for instance, ever' single night she'd set and rock in her rocking chair in front of the fireplace, rocking, spinning, sewing, stitching, spinning flax, or carding wool. Whatsomever she was a-doing, she'd do it for hours and hours, until she'd yawned real big three times. By then, she figured it was time to go to bed.

Now, she had a touch of the rheumatis', and she believed that fish oil cured it, so she kept nailed to the wall, alongside of the fireplace, a dried jack-salmon.² She'd cut off a chunk of that dried fish ever' night a-fore bedtime, and chaw on it till she felt better or fell asleep. She'd been at this so long that she'd begun to talking to the fish like he was one of the family, and calling him One-Eyed Jack,

95

being as how only one eye on him showed.

Word got out about this old widder-woman and all her cash-money, and it was bound to happen that three robbers come along and planned to rob her. The littlest, scrawny little robber was the scout, and the head robber sent him up to find the cabin. The next one was a short fat feller, he was to look out for the hounds, if'n the old woman had any, and the head robber was a big, burly feller, with a patch over one eye. He'd been a boatman, and a river pirate, and having only one eye, he'd come to be called One-Eyed Jack, same as the fish.

Onc't the scrawny little robber'd found the cabin, he couldn't find no place to look in, the winders's all shuttered up. Directly he found a place by the chimley where the chinking had fell out, and he could see in. He peered in through the chink, which happened to be right a-side the fireplace mantel, and just below the head of that old dried fish.

The old widder-woman was rocking and a-spinning, rocking and a-spinning, and she yawned real big. And she turned to the fish, her best friend, and announced, "There's one come. Two more comes, and I'll take my knife"—she looked right at that scrawny robber—"and take a slice out of you!"

Now, the little robber thought she was a-looking at him, clean through the chink-hole, and talking to him. He run like a rabbit back to the head robber, yelping, "That old woman must be a witch! She looked right at me, told me I was the first one to come, and two more'd come, and she'd cut a slice outen me!"

The head robber laughed, and called him a fool, and sent the little fat robber to spy out the house. The fat one found the chink-hole the same as the scrawny one'd done, and he peered in at the old woman. She was rocking and a-spinning, rocking and a-spinning, and she yawned real big the second time. She looked that fat robber right in the eye, right a-side the dried fish's eye, and declared, "Well, now, there's two come. One more comes, and I'll get my carving knife and take a chunk out of you!"

Now the fat robber become a believer! He took out a-running like a scared gander, and ran clean down to the head robber. "He's right," he said. "That old woman's a witch, sure. She seen me a-looking at her, she told me I was the second one to come, and when one more comes, she'll get her carving knife!"

One-Eyed Jack just laughed out loud. "I swear to my time," he growled, "this is the most cowardly bunch of robbers I ever fell in with. I'm a-going to go look at this old woman myself!" Well, he got to the cabin, and went to slipping around, and found the chink-hole right off. He stooped down a little, and peered in through the chink with his one good eye.

There sat the old woman, rocking and a-spinning, rocking and a-spinning, and she yawned the third time. "There's the third one come," she allowed, putting down her spindle, and picking up a carving knife off'n the table. She looked straight for that old fish, and the chink-hole a-side of it, and said to her best friend, "Now, Old One-Eye, I'm a-going to carve a slab out'n you!"

She et her fish, and she went to bed, and she didn't even know how that head robber'd passed them two little ones, and they didn't catch up to him till they was clean out of the county.

---

[1]Widow. This and many other words ending in *-ow* are pronounced as if they ended in *-er.*

[2]Jack-salmon is a male of the species, or a specific species of salmon, also called a walleyed pike, caught in the Ozarks.

Richard Chase collected an Appalachian version of this yarn called "Old One-Eye" in *The Grandfather Tales.* This Ozark variant was collected in fragments in 1985 and 1986, and reconstructed. Informant 24 was the principal informant, but gave no indication of when he had heard it.

The Six-Pound Crappie

27 **There's these boys standing around** in a circle, a-talking all about what good fishers they was. Bragging on who'd caught what and how big each catch was. Along come this old gent on a walking stick, and he struck up with 'em, and said: "Why, that's nothing, boys. I went out on the lake last year and took a six-pound crappie!"[1]

One old boy asked, "What in tarnation[2] was you a-using for bait?"

Old gent grinned and said, "A four-pound cricket!"

---

[1] A very small, fresh-water game fish. Pronounced "croppy."
[2] A prettied-up word for damnation.

Informant 20 told this anecdote in 1982. He did not say when he had first learned of the remarkable event.

The Blacksnake Lie

28 **A feller driv'**[1] **his wagon off'n the** road onto a lane, one day, and seen the most gigantical blacksnake he'd ever seen in his whole, born put-togethers.[2] The critter was easily as big around as a melon, and twenty foot long! But the most peculiar thing of all was the fact that the snake's tail was a-leading, coming toward the feller, with its head dragging along behind.

That old snake was a-coming straight at the wagon, tail first, and straight as you please, 'stead of twisting along the way a rightful snake oughta.

"P'rhaps it's been in the still,"[3] the feller said, to nobody in partic'lar. About then, the snake come alongside of the horse, who commenced to ramp and faunch.[4] Now, the feller leaned off'n the wagon to get a better look at the snake, and could see that the snake was stone cold dead, sliding along the lane back'ards, in a perfectly straight line. That done it! He whoa'ed his horse and got down, and walked along aside of this remarkable critter.

It was then that he observed that the snake was all bumpy, like as if he'd just et good. So he peered over closer, and seen that this partic'lar snake was leaving hoofprints. Now, you've heared the expression "lower than a snake's belly"? Well, this one's belly wasn't low enough, by about two inches. The feller flung hisself in the dirt and peered underneath. The snake had two dozen little black feet, like a woolly-worm with hooves.

About that time, a farmer come a-crashing out'n the timber, and durn near tripped on the feller and the snake.

"My sow had a litter three days ago and was out past the barn with her piglets," said the farmer, helping the feller from the wagon to get to his feet. "I just found her, and the litter's gone!"

The feller trod on the snake's head, and the thing snapped to a halt. The two men scratched their heads and studied on it a while, and directly took out an axe from the wagon and performed a axe-pendectomy on the snake.

Well, out come the missing piglets, eight of 'em, the source of the snake's recent demise being thirty-two sharp little trotters that had give it a bad case of the perforations. The pigs was no worse for wear, although just a touch indignant over the whole affair, and was obviously exceptional intelligent, even for pigs.

Since three-day-old pigs's not near raised-up enough to be out in the world without their ma, they'd been right on their way back to the barn.

The farmer was right proud[5] to have his litter back, and the feller with the wagon set out to home with a mind to take a different lane from then on.

---

[1]Past tense of *drive;* rhymes with *live.*
[2]Your entire natural life.
[3]Liquor distillery.
[4]To rave and chomp at the bit; *ramp* is also pronounced *romp.*
[5]Delighted.

Informants **8 and** 9 contributed this story, and a short version is found in the works of Vance Randolph.

What Are Friends For?

29 **The town rainmaker driv' up to** the forge one day and whoa'd his mule. He stood up in the wagon and hollered out to the smith:

"Smithy, I was wondering if you could drop by the house tonight and help me for a minute. It won't take very long, but I can't do it by myself."

"Sure," said the smith, "what're friends for? Whaddya need?"

"Well, if you'll drop by, you can help me get the mule out of the well."

"My stars," hollered the smithy, "the mule's in the well? I'll come right now!" The smith was ripping off his leather apron, and putting on his coat.

"Naw, naw . . .," says the rainmaker, "there ain't no hurry. She's been in there three days . . . She's just swelled up so, we can't get the bucket by her anymore."

Informant 10 told this story about his old nemesis, Informant 11. Informant 11 says it happened the other way around. At least one of them heard it as early as 1935. The two old friends take turn-about telling what a fool the other is, a common Ozark pastime.

Something's in the Chickens

30 **Friend of mine come up to the** house las' week and said, "I'm tard.[1] I'm worn completely out. You know, something's been a-getting at our chickens.

"We'd thought it was our neighbor Zeke for a long time, but Zeke don't leave nothing behind, and we kept finding feathers. So, finally, last night, Grampa got out the old double-barrel shotgun, put that powder down in there, poured a double handful of shot in each barrel, and said, 'I'm a-gonna get what's been a-getting my chickens!'

"Well, old Grampa put the shotgun above the door, and we all listened, but we didn't hear anything, so we all went on to bed. We slept sound for a full hour, and suddenly ever' chicken in the chicken house give tongue.[2] You never heard such a caterwauling in all your life. We all raised about a foot off the bed!

"Grampa, he beat ever'body to the floor; went a-ripping acrost there, simultaneously grabbed the doorknob and the shotgun, ripped that door open, and took off in his little nightshirt. He was barefoot; his little nightshirt don't even make his knee, and he ain't got nothing else on.

"Here he went, a-tearing off toward the chickenhouse, and old Trey the hound dog scrambled out from under the porch and took out behind him. The chickens's still a-raising Ned.[3]

"He got out to the chickenhouse door, cocked both hammers back on that shotgun, and eased that door open. He lifted up one foot to step over that doorsill, and about that time old Trey come up and cold-nosed Grampa from behind.

"Both barrels went off . . . and I been up all night a-cleaning chickens!"

---

[1]Tired.

[2]Gave tongue; made a lot of noise.

[3]Ned is the devil, and "raising Ned" implies a noise loud enough to raise the devil from hell to see what's the matter.

Several versions, in varying degrees of dialect, have come to the authors. The most perfect version is told by Informant 10. Informants 9 and 11 also tell it. It was heard as early as 1928 by the oldest of them. They often quarrel as to which one of them is the oldest.

My Day in Court

31 **When I drove a freight wagon, one** day I was driving along Main Street, making a goodly clip, with my mules galloping. But just as I rounded a corner, the Widow Wilson stepped out right smack in front of me, and I ran right over her wooden leg.

It scared her bad, but it didn't hurt her a-tall. Howsomever, it smashed her old wooden leg to smithereens. She was so mean, and so mad, she up and got the sheriff to take me to court as if it had been my fault.

In court she argued and caterwauled at the judge, but after he'd heard it all, the judge threw her out of court, of course.

She didn't have a leg to stand on.

Informant 11 tells this story, but who it happened to varies with each telling. Informant 10 also tells it, and they argue about who knew it first. Either way, they heard it as early as 1925.

Cracks in the Ground

32 **One awfully dry summer in up-**state Missouri, in the Missouri river valley, it got so dry that the ground cracked something terrible. One farmer took his tractor out and tried to cross one of the bigger cracks, and got the tractor stuck in the crack.

There was nothing to do but get off the tractor, go back to the barn, and get another tractor to pull the first one out. He was going to need a log chain to pull the first tractor out, so he threw it down by the edge of the crack.

Well, the hook-end was heavy enough that when it hit the ground too close to the crack, it slid right over and dangled down into the gap. In no time at all, the whole length had slithered over the edge and fallen into the crack. There was nothing to do but go back to the shed and get another chain.

When he got back half an hour later, with the second chain, he heard the first one hit bottom in the crack!

Informant 32 passed this tall one along in 1986. He said it really happened, of course, about fifteen years before that.

Old Shep

33 **This dairy farmer had the finest** help ever to come down the pike,[1] not a worthless hired hand, but the finest cattle-working dog there ever was! His name was Shep, and he was so smart, the farmer had known people that were stupider than Old Shep. Every night, when it was time to bring the cows to the barn, Old Shep would run up to the house and look at the clock to make sure it was time, and then run out to pasture and round them up to the gate, and sit there and count them as they went in. If one was missing, Old Shep would run back out to pasture and find her.

When every single cow was in, Old Shep would close the gate.

Then the farmer made a mistake. One of the neighbors came by and bought a cow, hauled her home right then, and the farmer neglected to tell Old Shep.

Shep came to the house that night, looked at the clock, ran to pasture, herded the cows home, and sat at the gate to count. One was missing! He ran back out to pasture, and couldn't find her anywhere! Poor Shep was frantic. He went to running around in gradually increasing circles, till he finally found that cow at the neighbor's barn.

Well, Shep got into the lot with her and nipped at her

heels to try to get her to jump the fence. The other farmer came out when he heard the ruckus, and told Shep it was his cow, and to leave her alone.

Shep didn't believe him for a minute, and just kept running around and barking at the cow. Finally, the farmer went back into the house, got the bill of sale, and let Shep read it.

Shep read through it twice before he gave up and went home.

---

[1]Road. The term *pike* is a holdover from when this tale was told in Kentucky, where it signifies any turnpike or good road.

Informant 18 told this Missouri version of the tale in 1983. The story seems to have come from Kentucky in about 1961.

Frightful Tales

Scary stories are most effective when told around a fire.

Mary Calhoun

3 4 **Onc't there came to these hills a** family by name of Calhoun. The old man was a-walking through the graveyard on a hilltop one Halloween about sundown. He sat down on a tombstone to rest for a minute, and when he got up to go, he left his walking stick there.

When he got to the cabin, he missed his stick and asked his eldest girl, Mary, to go and fetch it. She obliged, and walked up the hill in the dusky-dark, and through the iron gate into the graveyard. The stick had fallen over, kind of down into a crack where an old grave was caving in.[1] When she bent over to pick it up, something grabbed the hem of her dress.

She stood up sudden, too scared to scream, and something all bony and husky[2] climbed up her dress and onto her back. It was shriveled and hardly weighed a thing, and it spoke to her.

"Bear me out of here," said the thing into her ear. "I've not eaten a morsel in many a year!"

Mary tried to disobey, but she couldn't; she walked stiff-legged down the path toward the houses beyond the field.

"Turn in here," said the thing, as they come to a gate, then, "Nooo!" it wailed, "there's holy water here!"

"Turn in here," it hissed at the next gate, then, "Nooo! There's holy water here, too!"

"Turn in here," the thing said at the third house, and Mary done as it bade. "No holy water here!" it said. Mary knowed this house, and the folks that dwelt in it, and they had three fine sons. The thing on her back said, "Into the kitchen, and get a butcher knife." She found one. "And a bowl." She got one. "Upstairs," said the thing, and up she went, unwillt.[3]

There was the three sons, asleep in their beds. "Cut his throat," said the thing, and she done it, all unwonted. Out come three drops of blood into the bowl; the first one come and the boy stirred, the second one come and the boy was pale, the third one come and the boy was dead! She done the same to each; one, two, three.

"The kitchen," said the thing. She went down. "Build a fire," it said. She stirred the coals. "Make oatmeal," it said, "with the blood!"

When the oatmeal was b'ilt[4] with the blood, the thing bade her, "Set the table!" She laid out bowls and spoons. "Serve my supper!" She parceled out the oatmeal. "Take a bite!"

She lifted a spoonful of the bloody gruel, but her hand was a-shaking so hard, she dropped the morsel. It fell in the fold of her kerchief. "You're mine now," said the thing, and it climbed down and sat in a chair and commenced to eating its oatmeal. She dasn't[5] look at the thing; all dried up and powerful old. It ate, and ate. She done the same, but each bite she dropped into her kerchief when it wasn't looking. It couldn't bid her now, but she didn't let on.[6]

"Now you've et the blood," the thing said, chatty-like, "you're one of us. You can know all that we know; you'll never tell!" The thing put down its spoon and wiped its mouth. "If'n there'd been aught left of that oatmeal, it could've brung the boys alive again!" The thing laughed, and it sounded like wind in the cornshocks. "I've et," it

said. "Back to the grave!"

"I'll take up first," said Mary Calhoun, and she put the bowls and spoons in the basin, and folded her kerchief and laid it in the cupboard alongside the rags, as though she'd got it there; the thing took no heed.

"Up, now," said the thing, climbing her dress and setting on her back, "and to the grave." Onc't it had touched her again, the thing held sway over her, and she done as it bade.

To the grave they went. "See that cairn?" the thing said, "Under those stones I hid in life all the gold, ill-got, I had." The thing laughed, and it sounded like dry leaves in the wind. "Little it served me, but you'll not tell!"

They come to the grave, all caved in.

"Hurry," said the thing, "it's almost dawn!" The thing climbed off and crawled into the crack. Soon as it left her, it couldn't bid her. "Come down," said the thing.

"No!" said Mary Calhoun, taking up her father's stick.

"Come down!" said the thing. "You've et the blood!"

"No!" said Mary Calhoun. "Not a morsel!"

"Come down!" said the thing, and it grabbed ahold of her hem. She struck it with the stick, and sherds of it flew, but still it pulled.

"NO!" said Mary Calhoun, and a shaft of sunlight struck the crack as dawn came over the hilltop.

The thing let out a scream, and fell away into the grave.

Mary Calhoun went back to the house. The family was weeping and wailing over the dead boys.

"They're not dead," said Mary Calhoun. "They've swooned, is all. I'll take up a rag and a bowl of water."

"You're daft!" said the father. "They're dead!"

Mary Calhoun went up alone, with the oatmeal in the kerchief. She put one bite in each boy's mouth, then wet his brow as if to wake him. Each boy stirred, each boy swallered, each boy woke.

Mary Calhoun took her father's stick and went home.

114

Mary Calhoun never married; never had no children. She saved her pennies and bought the fallow by the hilltop. She come into some money; no one knew how. She made a fine house, and lived a long life, but she shunned the company of other folk, and she never, never, never entered the graveyard again.

---

[1]An old grave often caved in when the coffin in it collapsed; this was true of graves dug in haste, for example, out of fear or the absence of loved ones to dig a deep enough grave. By this one verb, the story implies that the dead man was either hated, feared, or alone in the world.

[2]Husk-like, dried out—not robust, as implied by modern usage.

[3]Unwilled, unwilling.

[4]Boiled.

[5]Did not dare to.

[6]By letting go of her, thinking she had eaten the gruel, the thing lost its power over her.

This tale has many variants, usually known by the name "Mary Culhane," that are Irish in origin. The dead thing from a grave climbing onto one's back and making demands is found in several tales recorded by William Butler Yeats. No single informant provided this story; the editors have heard many versions. Perhaps the finest version is told by Kathryn Windham, a southern storyteller. The story is said to come from Ireland, and is known to be over a hundred years old, at least. Yeats relates a story with a similar theme, wherein a corpse climbs on a wastrel, and demands to be carried to and buried in holy ground. Most settlers to the Ozarks were Protestant, and the presence of a more Catholic story—indicated by the Holy Water—gives interesting variety.

The Mo Mo

3 5 **Now, up in the woods of south New** Jersey, along the coast there, where the locals are called "pineys," they've got the New Jersey devil. Down south, you've got your skunk-ape. But there's not a monster around that can match up to what us hillbillies have seen—the dreaded Mo Mo.[1]

Now, Mo Mos get big. One feller up at Galena,[2] almost up to Crane, was over in the national forest west of Cape Fair, and came around a corner in a jeep, and his headlights hit something in the road right in front of him. It was Mo Mo! He can't describe him very well, though, except that he's big and black and hairy. If you ask about the critter's head, the feller just says, "I don't know. The headlights only reached up to its waist!"

They've been seen all over; in the late sixties in the wooded suburbs southwest of St. Louis, along the river, even over to Cape Girardeau, although I can't imagine why anyone, even a Mo Mo, would want to go there.

But the meanest, scariest Mo Mo was sighted around Mount Vernon in about 1959.[3] The feller that saw it told me he was coming back to the house from the fields just at dusk, and saw what he thought was a Negro farmer sitting in the unfenced field beside the road. As he got closer, he saw it was too big and too hairy to be a human being. It seemed to be sitting on its haunches, with its head in its hands, then it stood up abruptly!

It was about nine feet tall, and it strode across the road in front of the feller. It had long black hair all over it, and glowing orange eyes. When he got home, a lot of his chickens had been taken, and eaten in the field!

That's what Mo Mos do, they steal chickens. And they eat hogs. And they gut dogs, too. But they don't seem to eat the dogs.

So I guess they have some sense after all.

---

[1]Mo Mo is a name made up by the media, from the U.S. Post Office abbreviation MO for Missouri and another Mo for monster.

[2]Galena is the seat of Stone County, Missouri, but Crane is the more thriving metropolis.

[3]The dates and locations were tossed off casually, and probably wouldn't stand up in a court of law.

Informant 40 recounts this, and other Mo Mo tales, all of which he heard from the eyewitnesses themselves, in the 1970s.

The Hainted Car

36 **The preacher was setting in the** church house, long after ever'one else had gone home, waiting for the fire in the stove to die out, reading his Bible. It was cold and dark, and the wind howled around the old wood-frame church, banging the shutters. The preacher, he scattered the coals in the ash, turned the damper, and closed the stove; blew out the coal oil lamps and latched the shutters.

It was Halloween night; fell on a Sunday that year. Preacher swung shut the door to the church and turned the old iron key. Now, he weren't a superstitious feller, but he plumb shuddered in that wind as he pulled his coat up tight and commenced to walk down the rock road to the farmhouse where he was staying the night.[1]

He had to go over one hillock and through two hollers to get to where he's going, and on the hillock stood the graveyard. Down in the first holler, he thought he heard something on the road a-hind him. He stopped and turned to look, but there weren't no moon, and it was as dark as the inside of a cow. He walked on. A minute later, climbing toward the graveyard, he thought he heard something again. He stopped and turned back to listen. He couldn't hear no hooves, nor traces jangling, so he knowed it weren't no wagon. He couldn't hear no engine running, so he figured t'weren't no car.

He walked on, and just a-fore the edge of the graveyard, he heard it again—a low sound, like something horrible heavy, stalking him slow, crunching rock underfoot as it come. Something big and dark moved up the road at him, bigger'n a bear!

He backed a couple steps, then turned and was about to run for it, when the thing come up against the sky[2] and he seen it. It was a automobile, but 'thout its lanterns lit, moving slower'n he'd ever seen one move, and making no sound a-tall.

The hainted car come up on him slow, and stopped a-side him.

"Well," thought Preacher, "it's some deacon on his way back from taking some sister home, and he's offering me a ride!" He stepped up to the car, opened the door and got in, and leaned up to thank the driver.

The car was empty, 'cept for him.

Slowly, it commenced to move past the cemetery, no sound but the crush of gravels under its wheels. At the big iron gate to the graveyard . . . it stopped.

"Well," thought Preacher, "I guess this is where I get out!"

He climbed out of the car, and stepped aside to the gate, looking. All of sudden, he heard something a-hind the nearest stone, breathing hard and growly-like. Slowly, Preacher walked around the headstone. There stood a deacon of the church, panting and blowing like something was wrong with him.

"Brother Dan," said Preacher, "don't go near that car! There's something wrong about it!"

"I know, Brother John," said Brother Dan, "I been pushing the damn thing a mile!"

[1]Circuit-riding preachers were common in the Ozarks, staying with a different church family on each monthly visit to their several country churches.

[2]The car came up out of the hollow enough to be seen above the horizon of the previous hill.

This "ghost joke" came originally from Informant 4, but was said to have taken place in Texas. The Ozark version comes from several different informants, including Informant 22, from 1973 to 1978. It was first heard as early as 1957 by the editors, and at least some tellers claim it to be the truth.

The Creature in the Hole

3 7 **Down along the Buffalo River,** three teenaged boys were going swimming and deep diving. They went down to the river near the mouth of Hemmed-In Hollow.[1] There's a sharp bend in the river there, with a water-worn hole that's very deep. On the brightest days, the water looks black in that hole.

As they were swimming, they decided to dive down and see if there was a cave within the deep depression. It was late afternoon, and the sun was behind the bluffs. The hot sun and cold water had made wisps of fog in the cool coves. They were prepping for the dive, putting on their snorkels and fins, when an old woman walked out of the nearby woods, seemingly from out of nowhere.

She wore a very long skirt, and a blouse and vest, looking almost like a gypsy woman. She approached them and asked if they were about to go swimming. They said, "Yes."

"Haven't you heard," she asked, "about the Creature in the Hole?"

They answered that they had not.

"The stories have it that there is a creature that lives down there in that hole," she said. "Some say it's half-man-half-fish!"

The boys said that was a crazy idea.

"No," she answered, "investigate it yourselves. A few years ago[2] a diver went down to see for himself, and barely escaped with his life." She turned and left, as the boys were talking, and as they did not see her go, it seemed she had vanished.

After much discussion, they decided it was too late to dive that afternoon. No one would say he was scared, though.

The story could have ended there, except that several years later, some of the same young men took lessons in scuba diving from a prominent scuba diving school in southern Missouri. After the end of the lessons, there was a big party for all the students that had been enrolled. As they sat around eating doughnuts and drinking soft drinks, the tale of the Creature in the Hole came up. The instructor said, "That's an amazing coincidence. A diver I know from Springfield[3] went scuba-diving in a deep hole in the Buffalo River a few years back, and was attacked by what he described as a giant catfish. He just barely escaped with his life, and has scars on his leg to prove it."

---

[1]Hemmed-In Hollow is on the Buffalo National River in Newton County, Arkansas.

[2]The events happened, according to the story, in 1975. The ill-fated dive occurred in about 1971.

[3]Springfield, Missouri, is 120 miles north of the Buffalo site.

This story, and similar stories associated with the Creature, have circulated since the early 1970s, but this is the first time it has entered print. Informant 41 tells the story, a portion of which happened to him.

The Great Nothing

38 **When winter comes on, and the** winds blow cold and rustle the leaves across the ground, sometimes there comes a great stillness moving through the woods, down gullies and over ridges, up bluffs and across the river like a fog. It's such a stillness as'll wake the deepest sleeper. The owls don't hoot, the mice don't rustle in the walls. And the whole world gets silent and cold.

One dark night, without much moon, Paw was sitting downstairs in his rocking chair, and it was creaking on the puncheon floor. And Maw was a-knitting with her needles, and we could hear them clicking. And Old Brown, the hound dog, he was a-laying with his belly turned to the wood stove that glowed with a crackling log fire.

Us eight young'uns was upstairs in the loft, a-sleeping on our pallet. Now, with eight young'uns on a pallet that small, when one of us turned on our right side, all of us had to turn on our right sides. When one of us turned on our left side, all of us turned on our left sides, just like spoons a-laying in a drawer. The fit was tight, but on cold nights, ever'body kept warm.

On this one particular night, when we should've all been sound asleep, I woken up like a shot. Paw's chair wasn't creaking, Maw's needles wasn't clicking, and there wasn't a sound from Old Brown or the fire. My eyes flew open and I sat up. There wasn't a sound; it was still as the grave.

I couldn't even hear my brothers and sisters breathing next to me, for they was as wide-eyed as I was, and holding their breaths.

All of a sudden, we heared Paw rap on the loft ladder with the poker from the stove, and holler out my name, 'cause I'm the eldest. We all jumped at once, of course, there being eight of us in one bed, and the young'uns at the edges dodged the rafters and shakes.[1]

"Betty!" Paw hollered. "Betty, you look right now and count your brothers and sisters!"

So I crawled to the foot of the pallet and I commenced to count feet. There was two, then two more—and I counted off pairs of feet till I gotten to six. Me and six make only seven, and I knowed there was somebody missing. And I knowed right off who it was, too! Bear was the biggest of us, and he was missing.

So I turned to the loft hole and leaned down to say, "Bear's missing, Paw!"

"Bear's missing?" said Paw. "Where's Bear?"

We went to discussing how Bear could have gotten out of the loft without us knowing, since he had gone a-bed with all the rest of us. Paw went to rapping on the loft-floor for all us young'uns to get down that ladder, quick. Ain't nothing like a poker rapping under your bed to stir y' up!

Our clothes was our pillows, so we thrown back the quilts and hopped into our dresses and pants and things, and scurried down that ladder and lined up at the stove, from me down to the youngest. And we stood right up nex' to Maw, 'cause Maw was always safe. Her hair was down, and she was in her nightgown; she looked so purty, and young—and scairt.[2]

Bear was purt near Maw's favorite, being the oldest boy and all. He was tall, red-headed like maple leaves in fall, and so strong he could lift our wagon out of the mud all by hisself. All of us liked Bear, and even Mis'res Blount down to the schoolhouse liked Bear! If Bear was gone, we was all worried sick.

So Paw, he up and says, "I'm going out to look for Bear. You all stay here."

Paw put on his old coat, poked Old Brown with the poker, and he and the hound crept to the door and Paw opened it with a creak.

The silence outside almost knocked us down. Nothing was moving. Nothing was rustling. Nothing whispered, or murmured, or groaned. There was a fog on the ridge, and the whole world was frozen silent in it.

"Stay here with yer maw," says Paw, and out the door goes him and Brown, and the door closes with a thud.

We stood there by the stove, frozen without the cold, and nobody said a word. The door swung back open. "You all come on along, now!" barked Paw.

Maw turned white as flour, and you've never seen one woman move so fast in your life. She lined us children up and put us in our coats and hats, and we were right out that door in a line behind Maw, the baby closest to her and me bringing up the rear. We were in no shape to be left behind. Maw caught up to Paw and Old Brown, and all us chil'ren scrambled up close, like we was still sleeping in bed—walking in each others' footsteps, we was so close.

So Paw, Maw, and all us children walked along like a big woollyworm, with Old Brown snuffling along beside us. Me being the eldest, I was consid'rable taller than my next younger sister, so when Paw stopped and looked to the right, I looked to the left. When Paw looked to the left, I looked to the right. Then I saw Bear!

I went to tugging on my sister, who tugged on the next one, till the baby tugged on Maw's dress and Maw tugged on Paw's coattails. I just pointed to Bear.

"Stay put!" said Paw to Maw, and he walked over to Bear.

"Stay put!" said Maw to us children, and put we stayed.

Bear was hanging from a middling limb of a great big tree, hanging by his hands, his knuckles all white. Paw could just barely touch Bear's foot, he was hanging so high, like the wind taken him there. In the starlight and the moonlight, Bear's face was as white as school paper with no green lining on it. His eyes was rolled up white in his head, and his hair looked white in the light of the night.

Paw sent brother Randall up the tree, to pry Bear's fingers off the branch, and me and Paw tried to catch Bear as he fell. He didn't hit the ground too hard, and he didn't seem to mind, as he was just frozen, almost. So we all picked up Bear and carried him home.

Maw sent us all back up to bed, and she and Paw worked over Bear all night long, trying to get him awake. I don't think any of us remember sleeping that night, but when Paw pounded on the loft floor in the morning, we woken up, dressed, and come down the ladder quick as we could.

Maw lined us up, with me in the lead, and sent us to Granny's. I was plenty scairt, but on I marched, with all the others behind me—all but Bear. When we got to Granny's, Sally, the youngest, clumb up in Granny's lap, like we all wanted to. Almost all of us told Granny about Bear at the same time.

And Granny says, "Why, when I was a young'un, there was a great stillness like this that came over the land. Strange things happened to folks. And if any young'uns had told a lie, or thought a bad thought, or done an evil deed, or hadn't warshed behind their ears, why, this Great

Nothing creeps in along low to the ground and finds 'em if they're outside, 'cause they move when everything else is frozen so still. And it creeps up on you, and grabs you, and draws the warmth right out of you; all the warmth and all the goodness, just like that! But sometimes, if you're real strong, and there's more goodness than badness in you, you can fight it all off.

"So, all you children get busy!"

Granny helped us warsh behind our ears and clean our nails, and do the chores, and pack a lunchpail to take to Maw and Paw and Bear, and she sent us back home, marching acrost the hills all straight and tall.

When we got home and unwrapped the lunchpail, and Maw and Paw taken their nourishment and Bear had et, too, we all seen that he was better, but he was never quite the same again. Now, that Great Nothing ain't ever returned, but all us young'uns, we never go outside at night. At least, we don't go out until we've warshed behind our ears, cleaned our fingernails, and stood straight and tall in front of a mirror and said, "I ain't had nothing but good thoughts today, and I ain't told one single lie to anybody!"

And if that Great Nothing ever does come back, we'll be ready for it!

---

[1]Shake shingles, cut from oak.
[2]Scared.

This unusual tale has traveled an equally unusual path in the last century. It seems to be a cautionary tale for children that, judging from its motifs, originated in Germany. It came through the Ozarks a century ago, but apparently did not stay; the editors have never heard it in the Ozarks. The story went to Wyoming, where it was told by a grandmother to her daughter, who told her daughter, who moved to New Mexico, where it was told to our informant. This tale is retold from Teresa Pijoan de VanEtten, a native New Mexican storyteller and author of national prominence, who swapped it to the editors in 1988.

Smokey Joe

39 **On the banks of the Buffalo River,** there is a Boy Scout camp.[1] At that camp, some boys hear-tell a mighty strange story, and folks swear it's true!

They say . . .

Years ago[2] some boys were away from their tents, playing in the riverbed. They got to splashing each other, then throwing handfuls of mud, then someone got angry, and the mud started to include rocks. Just as a scoutmaster came along to break up the fight, the largest rock of all struck him hard in the side of the head.

The man went down hard, face down, in the riverbed. The boys were too scared to do anything, and ran for help. When they returned, he was gone. The man did not return to camp that season, in spite of extensive searches for him. At last the camp was closed up for the winter.

The next spring, with a new crop of Boy Scouts coming in, strange things happened. The doors to a food storage room were broken, as if by great strength. Things—primarily food items—disappeared from tent sites. Footprints were found . . . shadowy shapes were seen at night . . . and a mysterious lone silhouette was observed, high on the bluff across the cold, dark river, at the solitary tree known as Antenna Pine.

One day, a boy was out hiking alone, against camp rules, and began to climb the bluffs. He lost his footing and fell from one ledge height to a ledge below. He was knocked unconscious and suffered only a broken ankle.

When he regained consciousness, he was no longer on the ledge.

He found himself alone in a bluff shelter, high up the cliff-face over the river. The shelter was littered with cattle bones and food remains, and the area stank terribly. He climbed out as quickly as he could, and went down the cliff, hand-over-hand, to the camp.

In his haste and fear, he forgot the way back to the cave, and when questioned back at camp, was unable to tell exactly where he'd been. But his description of the smoked walls of the cave, and the smell, and the food leavings meant just one thing to the boys in the camp.

The boy had been rescued, thanks to the still-surviving instincts of the mysterious missing scoutmaster that the kids at camp call . . .

Smokey Joe.

---

[1]The camp, in Newton County, Arkansas, makes no claim concerning the story.

[2]This story has circulated since the late 1960s, and was first heard by the editors in 1969–70. That would put the alleged rock-throwing in the mid- or early sixties.

This story is well-known and circulated in a five-county area around the Boy Scout camp, and is variously sworn to be true and sworn to have been made up by some of the early tellers. This is the first time this yarn has entered print, and there are many variants and other recounted instances of Smokey Joe's actions. The man-creature's name may come from a "Smokey Bear" scout hat, or a campfire, or the smoked-up cave walls; tellers do not agree on this point. If the "graduates" of the camp have their way, Smokey Joe will enter American folklore as a familiar figure.

True Tales

The storytellers say these really happened.

Walker Rudd

4O **When old Brown's boy was a** young man, nineteen or twenty years old, it was the common practice on Saturday morning to load all the produce from their farm onto the wagon, hitch up the mule, and drive into Judsonia[1] to sell the crop for cash money. Brown's daddy didn't believe in them newfangled car inventions until a lot later on in life; if there was work to be done, he wanted a mule! They'd've loaded all their produce into the wagon, and drove into town to the Red Star feed-and-seed store, which still stood empty last time we looked.

They would take in their produce there, sell it, and with the cash money from the produce they would buy what they needed and haul it back in the wagon. Done that every Saturday.

This one particular Saturday, the family had loaded the wagon and was a-coming into town with the produce, and there was a crowd of folks at the loading dock of the feed-and-seed. Then Brown's boy looked up, and he chanced to see this old feller going down the road by the name of Walker Rudd. Now, Walker was the finest storyteller and windiest liar in the town of Judsonia. Nobody knowed what he done for a living—chawed tobacco, or something—but he sure could whip up a tale! Walker was making time up Main Street, walking along all intent and looking straight ahead.

Brown's boy hollered, "Hey—Walker. Come on over here and tell us a big old lie."

Walker kept on a-walking, looking straight on, "No—no—ain't got time!"

Brown's boy called out, "Oh, c'm'on, Walker, spin us a big old yarn!"

Walker stopped, turned around, put his hands on his hips, and said, "Dadgum it! I told you I didn't have time!" He said, "Bob Hulcey's just dropped dead!"

Ever'body on the dock looked up; they all knowed Bob.

"What?" said Brown.

"You heared me!" Walker said. "Bob Hulcey just dropped dead, and I'm on my way over there right now!"

Boy, ever'body on that loading dock turned around and throwed ever'thing into the wagons; took off for home. They didn't have to speak a word; ever'body knowed where ever'body else was going. Ever'body going to go home, clean up, change to their good clothes, get the womenfolks to put the available food under covered dishes, a-going to the Hulcey household and he'p the family. They'd load up feed for the animals, pine boards for the coffin; they's going prepared for two or three days.

Brown and them got home, dashed around, done all this and that, got on their good clothes, throwed the women-folks and ever'thing in the wagon, and took off for the Hulceys'.

It was seven miles over terrible road, bouncing around in that old mule-wagon; took 'em the better part of an hour to get there. Finally got there, pulled in, looked: there was Bob Hulcey! He's out in the pea-patch, a-picking peas and squeezing bugs, and he looked pretty good for a dead man.

Now, Brown was a little-bitty feller; he was short, but he'd worked as a lumberjack all his life, and he was stout. He was huffing and puffing like a little old steam engine; hopped down off that wagon, walked over there, grabbed the garden gate, tore it just about off its hinges trying to get through it. Walked up behind Bob Hulcey, said, *"Bob!"*

Bob nearly jumped out of his skin; he didn't know nobody was there. Said, "Brown! What're you doing here?"

Brown, looked him up and down, and said, "Bob—are you all right?"

Now Bob's an old man, but he's obviously fine.

Bob kind of felt of himself, looked around, and said, "Yeah. I'm fine! What d'you want?"

"Never mind," Brown barked, "I'll be back and explain it to you later!" He walked back over, kicked what was left of the garden gate out of his way, jumped in the wagon, and took off. They're going to Walker Rudd's house.

They made it in record time; pulled into the yard, looked, and there sat Walker Rudd up on the front porch, leaned back in a straight chair. He had his thumbs in his galluses; he was waiting for 'em. Brown hopped down off that wagon and strutted like a little banty rooster up to the front porch.

"How come you to tell us Bob Hulcey just died," Brown rasped, "and we just drove all the way over there, and he's out there in the pea patch picking peas?"

And Walker said, "Now, Brown, if you'll just recollect, that boy of yours hollered at me as I was a-going along the street there in Judsonia, and asked me to tell him a big old lie!" Said, "I was in a hurry right then . . . and that was the biggest one I could think of on short notice!"

---

[1]Judsonia, Arkansas.

Informant 8 recounted this true yarn in 1982. He heard it from his father in about 1964; it is said to have happened in the 1930s.

The Warshboard

41 **Once there was this old boy from** LeFlore County[1] used to show off his wife, and say, "Doesn't look like she's missed a meal in her life, does it?" And we'd laugh, and he'd say, "Well, I tell you, there's a good reason for that.

"The day we got married, I took my lovely wife to the hardware store, and bought her some lovely presents. I bought her a warshtub and warshboard, and I bought her a mirrer.

"I told her she could take the warshboard and the warshtub, and get right to work, or she could use that store-bought mirrer and watch herself starve to death."

---

[1]LeFlore County is in east central Oklahoma.

Informant 15 told this anecdote in 1983. His wife swears it happened in about 1955.

Grandpa Skinned the Squirrels

42 **You're not going to believe this,** but my grandpa went out hunting every day. He'd shoot anything he could get; he had twelve kids, he had to shoot something. Squirrels, rabbits, blackbirds—whatever. He had a little lean-to right on the back of the house, and Grandpa used it for very little else 'cept cleaning what he'd killed. All he needed was a warshbasin and a good, sharp knife.

He'd get out there, and he'd skin up and clean out and fix up ready to go in the pan, whatever he'd shot.

Now, the hounds knew what was going to happen when Grandpa went into the lean-to. It had a window, with no glass or screening, and the hounds would go and sit right outside it. As Grandpa got whatever it was cleaned up, he'd toss head, liver, lights,[1] and all out the window to the dogs.

As the remains came flying out, the dogs'd just get under them, catch 'em out of the air, and swallow 'em whole.

One day Grandpa was out there doing what he usually did, skinning some squirrels. He skinned the first one, and threw the leavings to the dogs. Skinned the second squirrel, fed the leavings to the dogs. Now about this time, there was a little knot-headed barn cat, about five weeks old, under the bench there, trying to get a share of all this

carnage. He was catching at the leavings with his claws as Grandpa'd swing 'em for the window.

On about the third big swing-by with squirrel remnants, the cat latched on with his claws. But Grandpa was a lot stronger than the cat, and out the window went the cat with the squirrel parts!

The oldest hound paid no heed to what was in the air, and swallowed the cat and the squirrel in a single gulp.

The hound's eyes got wide. He stiffened up. His hair stood on end.

And in one swoop, as quick as he'd swallowed it all, it all came right back up, the barn cat yowling and clawing. The cat shot across the yard and disappeared into the hay.

From that day forward, the oldest hound never caught leavings on the fly anymore. He'd let it hit the ground, and take a right good look at it, and stir it around with one paw, before he'd eat a bite.

---

[1]Lungs.

Informant 44 told this tale in 1987, and swears it's the truth. It is said to have happened in Knoxville, Arkansas, in the '20s, according to her grandfather.

The Snooty Girl's Dream

4 3 **There was this little girl walking** down the hill from the barn, going to town, balancing a bucket of milk on her head. She was walking along, talking to herself, and daydreaming snooty dreams.

The little girl said, "I'm going to take this bucket of milk that I got from Daddy's cow, take it to town and sell it, and I'm going to buy me some hatching eggs. I'm going to hatch them eggs, and that'll get me some chickens, and they're going to lay more eggs, and that'll get me more chickens. And I'm going to do that a bunch of times, and when I've got enough chickens, I'll sell them all and buy me a pig.

"And I'll get that pig fed up so big and fat I can sell her at the market, and take that money and buy me the prettiest red dress that's ever been seen at any play party[1] anywhere!

"And I'm going to dance with that pretty party dress on, and all the boys are going to say, 'Ooooh . . .,' and then they're going to come over and ask me to dance.

"And when they ask me to dance, I'm going to say, 'No!' "

And when she said "No!" she flipped herself under the chin,[2] and her head went back, and the bucket of milk fell in the dirt. She didn't get to sell her milk, didn't get any

139

chickens, didn't get a pig, didn't get a pretty party dress. Which just goes to prove that snooty dreaming snooty dreams always come to no good.

---

[1]A play party is a social gathering at which games are played that involve singing, clapping, and rhythmic movement. No musical instruments are present, so church admonitions against dancing are not violated. Ozark dances almost always involved liquor, and often ended with some form of fighting or violence; families that did not dance would sponsor play parties the same nights as the big barn dances.

[2]Flipping under the chin is a capricious gesture, made by brushing the tips of the fingers outward from under the chin, with the palm toward the breast. It connotes rejection of flirting advances.

Informant 19 told this tale in the summer of 1984. She had known it half her life . . . since about 1978.

Let's Break Jack

44 **Now Daddy, he was an inventor.** Didn't get no credit like 'at Edison feller, but was really something. Anything he needed, he'd just make up something that'd work. He invented the firs' electrical fence in Illinois!

Y'see, we had this old mule, that'd worked in the fields for years, and was getting ornery and smart. He didn't like being penned up, and he loved breaking down fence-rows. Old Jack could sidle up to the fence, slide his eyes to the left and the right to see if there was anybody watching, and then put his chest up against a fencepost and lean on it. He'd lean on it till it started to lean, and he'd move his hooves up and lean a little harder, till 'e broke the fencepost off.

It was about to drive us all to distraction, when Daddy was a-watching Jack leaning on a fencepost one afternoon, and said to us, "Boys, let's break old Jack of that habit! One of you run out to that Model T Ford, and bring me the coil out of it."

In just jig time[1] we had a fence-wire strung up around the inside of the fencerow of Jack's pen. With the coil set up, we went into the house to watch. Now Jack he done his usual trick. He sidled up to the fence, looked both ways, and leaned onto 'at fencepost, real casual-like.

Old Jack hit 'at wire, and jumped into the air. His tail bushed out like a bottle-brush, his eyes got wide, he spun around and ran to the middle of the field, where he stood for the rest of the afternoon, a-snorting and a-shaking his head, wondering how they'd made that fence jump out and bite him.

And after that, we didn't set no more new fenceposts till I was grown.

---

[1]With great speed, as in dancing a fast-footed jig.

Informant 42 told this tale in December 1984, swearing it had happened in about 1925.

Rabbit for Lunch

45 **Trapping rabbits for their hides** was a paying business for plenty of young men in Oklahoma. One boy was on the way to the schoolhouse, and passed a rabbit in one of his traps. He didn't want to leave him there 'cause some critter'd come and eat him, so he knocked him in the head, and put him the only place he could think of, the bottom of his flat metal lunchbox, under the gravy tray. All he had was cornbread and gravy anyways, so he just dropped the cornbread into the chicken-gravy, and there was plenty of room left for the rabbit.

Things at school went along pretty good, till about eleven o'clock, when the lunchbox commenced to jumping around on the shelf over the coatracks.

At first the teacher thought somebody was making the noise, whilst she was a-teaching math, but pretty soon she seen it was Johnny's lunchbox.

"Johnny," said the teacher, real stern, "what-a you got in your lunchbox?"

"Uh . . . that ain't my lunchbox, ma'am," said Johnny.

Right then, the box give a special big jump.

The teacher marched right back to the coatracks, and touched the latch on the box.

Out jumped this gravy-soaked rabbit, springing over the teacher, scaring her half to death, and she fell flat on her back, bawling like a heifer.

All the girls went to standing on their desks, and all the boys went to chasing 'at blamed gravy-covered rabbit all around the room. The teacher was a-yelling, the girls was a-screaming, and the boys was a-laughing! What a commotion!

Lastly, the rabbit made it to the door, which was open a hair, and shot out the door like a bullet.

The teacher got to her feet, and said, "Johnny! Why'd you bring 'at rabbit to school?"

"It wadn't my rabbit," Johnny blurted out, and added, "and who's going to pay me the six bits I'd-a got for it?"

Informant 16 told this tale in 1986. He claimed it had happened about 1945 in eastern Oklahoma.

The Pallet on the Floor

46 **There was this young couple from** the city, who went to visit some shirttail cousins[1] in the hills, whom they'd never met before. They stayed up late talking and reminiscing about mutual acquaintances and relatives, and as the young'uns got sleepy, they climbed on the big old bed and fell asleep.

When they'd slept about half an hour, the ma would lay out a pallet[2] on the floor near the fire and transfer the sleeping young'uns into it. The teenagers did the same; fell asleep on the bed. The pa had to h'ist up the biggest boy to get him into the second pallet, on the other side of the hearth-rock.

Finally, the old folks said to the young couple, "You'ns can sleep in the big bed tonight, being's how yo're comp'ny."

So the city kids undressed down to their skivvies, and climbed into the big bed under the comforter.

But when they woke up the next morning, the old folks were in the bed, and the city kids were in a pallet right in front of the fire!

[2]One or two quilts, folded to the right length or width, used as padding on the floor—with as much cover as weather calls for added on top of the sleeper.

Informant 22 tells this story frequently, and swears it's true. He says it happened in the 1940s.

Uncle Marcus and the Panther[1]

4 7 **About seventy-five years ago, when** Pa and Uncle Marcus was young'uns, there was this little old lady used to come to visit Granny, and bring her youngest along to play with my kin. Along about sundown, she always liked to have a drink of fresh[2] spring water, and Granny sent the neighbor boy and Uncle Marcus along to fetch it. They took[3] four buckets, and Uncle Marcus took along a club-stick in case they met up with any panthers— which was highly unlikely, but it made Uncle Marcus feel right good to have it along.

Well, they was supposed to carry two buckets each, but Uncle Marcus was a powerful talker, and purt[4] soon, he had the neighbor boy a-carrying all four buckets, and him the club, smacking it into his palm and rattling on about panthers and how dangerous they was.

Now, Pa heared 'em leave out, and heared Uncle Marcus going on[5] about panthers, so he took his panther whistle[6] and laid out along the hedgerow on the path to the spring to wait for 'em, knowing his brother'd talk panthers ever' step of the way.

Directly, they come back along the path, Uncle Marcus holding forth[7] on the perils of panthers, and the neighbor boy lugging all four buckets of spring water. Pa showered

down[8] on that panther whistle hard, and Uncle Marcus said, "Li—"

Didn't even get the whole word "listen" out, and they took off a high-tailing[9] it to the house. When they shambled up to the porch, puffing and blowing, Marcus had dropped the club and the neighbor boy had a half-inch of water in one bucket—and three bails.[10]

Onc't Granny got wind of it, Pa laid out[11] two days over that'n!

---

[1]Pronounced like *painter* in pure Ozark dialect.

[2]Implies cool, in this sentence.

[3]Pronounced *tuck* in pure Ozark dialect.

[4]Pretty, meaning fairly.

[5]Carrying on; continuing to talk ramblingly.

[6]A hand-carved wood whistle that imitates the scream of a panther.

[7]The same as *going on.*

[8]To blow hard and wetly.

[9]Hurrying. Whether the term refers to the raised tail of the frightened white-tailed deer, or the tendency of dogs to raise the hindquarters higher in a hard run, is much debated around fireplaces in the Ozarks.

[10]Only the wire bails—the handles—remained in his hands; he had lost the buckets in his frantic run.

[11]Stayed away from home, to avoid a scolding.

Informant 22 told this true tale in 1974. It happened in the Ouachitas in 1928 or 1929.

The Pretender's Ghost

48 **Two men got in a fight over a girl at** a barn dance, and one took up a shovel from among the implements there, and killed the other with repeated blows. The killer fled from the barn, and was not seen again for quite some time.

The law was laying for him[1] but couldn't seem to come by him.[2] About that time, an old house that had stood abandoned was seen inhabited again, but no one out on the lonely road questioned that, since the owners' family came and went. One woman, always dressed in the same light cotton housedress and a long slat bonnet,[3] was seen about the yard of the old place, at the well, and such.

Finally the sheriff got wind[4] that the odd-looking woman was the killer, hiding out in the vacant house, who only came out pretending to be a woman. The house was surrounded in short order[5] and the killer shot it out with the law. The murderer was gunned down, and his body taken out of state.

Not long after that, the old house burned to the ground mysteriously, and the owners never rebuilt it.

Over the next few years passers-by at dusk or cloudy-dark times claimed to have seen a ghostly figure of a woman in a light cotton house dress and pale slat bonnet,

wandering in the empty yard at the old well.

---

[1]Constantly watching for him, to capture him in ambush.
[2]To get ahold of, to apprehend.
[3]A slat bonnet has a long visor that covers the face almost completely.
[4]To hear by rumor.
[5]Quickly.

Informant 35 lived a short distance from the house-place, and tells this story as the truth. It took place, he said vaguely, in the 1970s.

The Old Hen's Kittens

49 **There was this man what owned** this crossroads general store. Anything you wanted or needed you could buy there, and he also had this big black momma-cat for catching mice and sleeping in front of the wood stove like a picture postcard. Momma-cats are good at that. After a while, the old cat come in with four baby kittens. They're good at that, too.

The kittens was black as coal, and sleek as weasels, and just about the time they opened their eyes, something happened to the old momma-cat. She up and died. The man what owned the store got right stubborn about the kittens. He needed one cat, for sure, so he got set on raising the whole litter up.

He had every kind of bottle and thing, and right quick-like he found a way to feed them. But the kittens cried and cried. He got them all fed good, and put them in a box, up on the molasses barrel, right next to the wood stove, where it was warm, but they cried and cried.

Finally, the man got desperate, and went out and got an old setting-hen, and set her right smack in on those kittens. The hen fluffed around a little bit, and looked powerful close at those kittens, but right soon she settled down on them, and the kittens went straight to sleep.

Directly, folks coming into the store started asking what the hen was for, and the spit-and-whittle crowd around the stove took great delight in teasing the folks, saying, "Lift her up and see!"

Well, folks would lift the old setting-hen, and everyone would have a good chuckle over it all.

This went on for several days, when there come to town a little shirttail[1] young'un, who wandered into the store and right quick wanted to know why the old hen was setting in the store. Now, he wasn't tall enough to see the top of the barrel by himself, much less lift the old setting-hen, so one of the loafers picked him up, and another hoisted up the old hen.

The boy looked at the kittens, and grinned, and looked at the hen, and looked back at the kittens, and back at the hen, and by the time the loafer had set him down, his lip was a-quivering.

The boy headed for the door, tears running down his dirty face, sweeping the floor with his shirttail.

Well, those loafers couldn't stand it, and one of them asked, "Wha-jou[2] think of them kittens?"

The boy busted out crying.

Well, those old boys were pretty nigh dead of curiosity, and couldn't bear to see the young'un cry, so they gathered all around him and one of them asked, "What's wrong?"

"Mister," said the young'un, "I ain't sure . . . but I believe I've done et my last egg!"

---

[1] Youngsters wore nothing but their pa's old shirts up to the age of ten or so, and often had no real pants until almost reaching puberty.

[2] "Wha-jou" for "what did you" marks the story as coming from near the western border of Missouri, close to Kansas.

In the Ozarks most stories of this type end with some closing lines to soften the ending or make everything "come out all right." One would expect this story to end, "They took him up in a lap and explained it all, fine," as some similar stories do. The absence of such an ending seems to indicate that this story is, in fact, true. Informant 37 told this story in May 1984 as the truth, but gave no date for the event.

Jokes

Many Ozarkers say "joke" for any story that has a pleasant ending.

There Ain't Been No News

5O **Once there was a man down in** Fort Smith, Arkansas, that ran a "feed, seed and everything you need" store, but in order to do his business he traveled a lot by train. When he'd go away he'd get his cousin Fred to look after the farm chores for him. Well, he was gone for weeks one time, and came home, and he'd wired Fred to meet him at the station.

"Fred," he said when he saw him, "what's the news?"

"Oh, Henry," said Fred, "there ain't been no news."

"You mean to say there ain't been no news, and me gone for weeks?"

"Nope," said Fred. "There ain't been no news. Oh . . . except your dog died. But other than that, there ain't been no news."

"My dog died?" said Henry. "What happened to him?"

"Well, that's easy to explain," said Fred. "He ate too much burned horse meat. But other than that, there ain't been no news."

"Wait a minute," said Henry. "Where'd my dog get ahold of burned horse meat?"

"Well, that's easy to explain," said Fred. "When your barn burned to the ground it killed all your livestock, and your dog got ahold of too much burned horse meat, and died.

But other than that, there ain't been no news."

"My barn burned?" said Henry. "What caused my barn to burn?"

"Well," said Fred, "that's easy to explain. It was sparks. Sparks from the house set the barn ablaze, and killed all your livestock, and your dog got ahold of too much burned horse meat, and ate it, and died. But other than that, there ain't been no news."

"Sparks from the house?" said Henry. "What happened to my house? Did my house burn down?" Fred was nodding solemn-like. "What burned my house down?"

"Oh, Henry, that's easy to explain," said Fred. "It was the candles, they set the curtains on fire. All them candles around the coffin. They set the curtains on fire and burned the house down, and sparks from the house set the barn ablaze, and the barn burned down and killed all your livestock, and your dog got ahold of too much burned horse meat, and died. But other than that, there ain't been no news."

"What coffin?" hollered Henry, lifting Fred off the landing by his lapels. *"Who died?"*

"Now, Henry," said Fred, "that's easy to explain. Your mother-in-law died, and we had the wake in the parlor, and the candles set the curtains on fire and burned the house down, and the sparks from the house set the barn ablaze, and burned the barn down, and killed all your livestock, and your dog got ahold of too much burned horse meat, and ate it, and died. But other than that, there ain't been no news."

"WHAT HAPPENED TO MY MOTHER-IN-LAW?" yelled Henry, shaking Fred around in the air.

"Oh . . . Henry . . . we've been arguing about that. Some says one thing and some says another. But as near as we can figure, she died of a broken heart when your wife ran off with the seed clerk.

"But other than that, there ain't been a bit of news!"

No single informant provided this Ozark version of a well-known Appala-chian tale. There are many variants of it, including fragments told to the authors by informants from three states. The best Appalachian versions were independently collected by Richard Chase and by Barbara Freeman and Connie Regan-Blake. The feed store motif appears only in the Ozark version. Informants 20 and 22 and others tell it in joke form.

What the Doctor Said

51 **The old woman of the house come** in to the parlor, and looked at the old man of the house, sitting in his rocking chair, and said, "Is there something the matter with you? You ain't stirred out that door in three solid days!"

"Well," he said, "I don't feel bad, but I don't feel right pert." So she up and took him to the doctor.

After the doctor had examined him, he sent the old man out to the waiting room, and talked to the old woman.

He said, "Now, we can get him out of this, but you've got to do three things: cook him three good meals a day, see to his ev'ry need, and wait on him hand and foot."

The woman said, "What'll happen if I don't do all that?"

The doctor said, "He'll likely die!"

The old woman went out to the waiting room.

"What'd the doctor say?" asked the old man.

"He said you'll likely die!"

Informant **7** provided this joke in 1985, but gave no indication of when she had learned it.

The Jumping Mules

Down there in LeFlore County,[1] they hunt a lot of raccoons in the Kiamichis,[2] but the country is rugged enough that they hunt 'em on muleback; can't hunt 'em on foot.

One day this old boy went out to buy himself one of them slim, trim, fence-jumping mules. His daddy liked the little critter so much, he went out and bought himself one, too. Soon as the daddy got home, they knew they had a problem, 'cause they couldn't tell them little mules apart!

They took them mules out in the yard, and looked 'em over. The daddy got a measuring stick and measured both them little mules, from the ground to the point of their shoulder, and both of them was exactly fifty-one inches tall. Couldn't tell 'em apart.

They drug out the balance scales and weighed 'em. Both them little mules weighed exactly seven hundred and fifty pounds apiece. Couldn't tell 'em apart!

They took 'em both back to their stalls, and the daddy got an idea and said, "You know, if one of us was to roach the mane on his mule, we could tell 'em apart." The son studied on it awhile, and it sounded like a good idea. So the son roached his mule's mane off. When he came out of the stall, he ran into his daddy carrying his mule's mane.

Couldn't tell 'em apart!

Finally, in utter desperation, they decided to measure them mules again, this time from front to back. Sure enough, they found out that the little white mule was a good two inches longer than the little black mule!

---

[1]LeFlore County is in the fringes of the Ozark Plateau in east central Oklahoma, across the border from Fort Smith.

[2]The Kiamichis are the hills just west of the Ouachitas and southwest of the Bostons, at the very edges of the Ozark Plateau.

Informant 15 told this story in 1982. He swears it is true, but dozens of other variants indicate that, if it's true, it is a surprisingly common event. Informant 1 told a version as early as 1950.

The Three Little Pigs Go to School

53 **The old momma pig and the three** little pigs was all living together in a little house, and the momma pig began to fret that her young'uns were growing up ignorant. So she sent them to pig school.

After their first day in school, she asked the oldest piglet, "What did you learn in school today?"

He said, "Oink, oink-oink, oink-oink-oink."

"Oh," said the momma pig, "I knew you'd be good in math."

Then she turned to the middle pig, and said, "What did you learn in school today?"

The middle pig said boldly, "Oink *oink*, oink *oink* oink-oink!"

"My, my," said the momma pig, "Shakespeare!"

And she came to the last pig, and said, "And what did you learn in school?"

The little pig said, "Arf, arf-arf!"

"What did you say?" asked the momma pig.

"Arf, arf-arf," said the little 'un.

"What 'n the world is that?" she asked.

"Foreign language!"

Informant 7 related this educational epic in 1985.

Carnation Milk

The Carnation Milk Company, that puts up the condensed milk in the little red cans, decided they was going to have a promotion amongst all the farm women that lived in one area where they bought milk to can. They was going to offer a big prize to whatever woman could write down the best poem about Carnation Milk, and mail it in to them.

Well, there was one little old woman out on a farm decided she'd enter the contest. She thought and she thought, and she finally came up with what she knew—just knew—was a winner! So she wrote down on a postal card,

> "Carnation Milk comes in the little, red can;
> It's the very finest milk in all of the land."

And she addressed it and give to her hired hand to put out in the mailbox.

Time went by, and the old woman was waiting—just waiting for 'em to come and give her the prize. She didn't hear from 'em in a coon's age, and she begun to get suspicious. She finally went out after a month had passed, and she confronted her hired hand. She said, "Did you mail that postal card I give you with the poem on it?"

He said, "Yeah, I did."

She said, "Well, I ain't heared[1] from them people, and I just knew I'd win." She looked at him, and she said, "Di'jou[2] make any changes in my poem?"

And he said, "Well, ma'am, yeah, I actually did. I have to confess, I read what you had writ down, 'Carnation Milk comes in the little, red can; It's the very finest milk in all the land,' and I just looked at it and said, 'Now, that ain't really nothing special 'cause it don't really get to the heart of the matter.' So I added a little bit onto it."

She said, "Well, what did you add?"

And he said, "Well, I added two more lines:

'No tits to pull, no hay to pitch;
Just poke a hole in the son of a bitch!' "

---

[1]The use of *ain't,* with the subject first person singular, meaning "I haven't," is correct in the Scottish dialect of English and is common among the Scots-Irish descendants in the Ozarks.

[2]*Di'jou* is phonetic for "did you," as pronounced in the South and Midwest.

Informant 21 told this joke-tale in 1981. She claimed it was true, and gave no date for the notorious event.

Foot, Footfoot, and Footfootfoot

5 5 **Three rabbits lived in a house at** the foot of the hill: Foot, his son Footfoot, and the grandson Footfootfoot. They was a little slow on names in their family. Now Foot said to Footfoot and Footfootfoot, "Footfoot and Footfootfoot, I'm an old gray hare, and my time has come!"

Sure enough, Footfoot and Footfootfoot looked at Foot, and he was a-turning pale. So quick like a bunny rabbit, Footfoot and Footfootfoot took Foot to see the foot doctor. Of course.

Well, the foot doctor confirmed to Footfoot and Footfootfoot that Foot was not long for this world. Soon afterward he expired, leaving the family footless. They buried him in a one-foot coffin one foot deep beside the footpath, and set a footstone on the grave. Of course.

The little house at the foot of the hill wasn't the same without Foot, and one day Footfoot said to Footfootfoot,

"Footfootfoot, I don't feel a-tall well."

They left the little house at the foot of the hill, hot-footed down the footpath past Foot's footstone to the foot doctor, and the foot doctor looked at Footfoot, and said to Footfootfoot, "Footfootfoot, I may not be able to save Footfoot."

"Oh, Doc," said Footfootfoot, "you've got to save Footfoot. I've got one Foot in the grave already!"

Informant 7 told this footloose tale in 1985. We understand that Footfoot did survive, at least in this footnote.

The Skunk Brothers

🐾

5 6 Once upon a time, there was two little-bitty baby skunks. One was named Out, t'other was named In. Whenever they was home, Out spent most of the time out, and In was almost always in. But sometimes In went out and Out came in. And if In was out and Out was in, and In came in, Out went out.

One fine day, In was out and Out was in, and their mother came to Out and said, "Out, your brother In has been out too long. Go out, Out, find In and bring In in."

He understood perfectly, of course, and in no time at all, Out came in, bringing In in with him.

"Outstanding, Out!" said their mother. "How did you find In out there so fast and bring In in, Out?"

Out just smiled, and said, "Instinc's!"

Informant 7 told this joke in 1985.

Smackout

5 7 **Up in Webster County,[1] down in the** hills, right on the Douglas County line, sat the little old town of Smackout. You could chuck a rock out the back of the general store and hit Douglas County, it was so close. These two elderly ladies run the general store, which is where the name of the town come from: them women hardly ever kept more'n a wheelbarrow-load of groceries in the store at any given time. Like as not, you'd walk in 'ere and ask for som'thing, and they'd answer, "No, we ain't got none. We're smack out."

Well, some city criminals hid out in the hills some y'ars back, and they got to counterfeiting money to pass on the locals. They got carried away one day, and went and printed 'em up a whole raft[2] of fifteen-dollar bills by mistake. The boss come in and said, "What-a-ya done?[3] We ain't never gonna[4] get shed of[5] these fifteen-dollar bills!"

The little robber, who was a mite smarter than the rest of 'em,[6] said, "Naw, in some of these little towns around here, people ain't got no better sense. I will pass them fifteen-dollar bills myself."

He went out the door with a bunch of them in his pocket, hopped on his mule, and rode straight for Smack-out.

Got there, walked right into the general store, went right back to the candy counter and got himself thirty cents' worth of candy. Walked right up to the cash register and whopped that candy down[7] and the old lady said, "That'll be thirty cents."

Well, he handed her one of them fifteen-dollar bills.

She didn't bat an eye. She punched up thirty cents on that old cash register, popped that old drawer open, rang the bell, and handed him back two seven-dollar bills and two thirty-five-cent pieces.

---

[1] Webster County is in Missouri.

[2] A jumble or pile.

[3] "What-a-ya done" for "what have you done" implies a flatlander from the Midwest instead of a hillbilly talking.

[4] Phonetic for the Midwestern "going to"; hillbillies would more likely say "going 'o," pronounced "go-win-uh."

[5] Rid of. Here the narrator slips into Ozark idioms instead of the Midwestern speech the head counterfeiter was speaking.

[6] There are always three robbers or criminals: the boss, the brute, and the little guy who is the brains of the operation.

[7] The repetition of the word "right," and the verb "whopped," imply brazenness on the part of the little robber. Ozark yarn-spinners choose their words carefully to paint the picture, and often use sound effects and onomatopaeia hard to duplicate in print.

Informant 25 told this story in 1980. He's been telling it since the 1920s.

Your Ma Says "Hullo"

58 **One time, 'is[1] big Ozark feller was** a-going to New York City for something, and a old widder-woman said to him, "My son lives in New York. If'n you'uns see him, say 'hullo.'"

"What's his name?" as'd the big feller.

"Name's John Dunn," said the old woman.

"I'll sure do it," said the big old boy, and he got on the train at Springfield[2] and went to New York.

Whilst he was in New York, he come on this big old building said Dun & Bradstreet on it. So he went in. He come up to 'is secretary, and asked, "Have you got a John here?"

She directed 'im to the warshroom. "Two doors down, on the left," she said.

So he went down there, and went in, and met 'is feller a-coming out.

"Are you Dunn?" he asked the city feller.

"Yes," said the city slicker, "I'm done!"

"Well," said the Ozark boy, "your ma says 'hullo.'"

[1]Abbreviation of *this*.
[2]Springfield, Missouri.

Informant 7 passed this one along in 1986, but she seems to have heard it very shortly before that, and from a flatlander!

The Seventeen-Minute Sermon

59 **Onc't there was a preacher 'at** preached a seventeen-minute sermon. You could depend on it! Not a sixteen-minute sermon, not an eighteen-minute sermon; a seventeen-minute sermon. Right at seventeen minutes, he'd holler 'amen,' and ever'body'd go home. Word got out quick; you never got out of church late, you was always on time for dinner, the young'uns never got cranky. Folks begun to flocking to the church in droves.

The church was full; the preacher was happy. The collection plates was full; the deacons was happy.

And the secret was . . . a cough drop! He'd bounce up to the pulpit to preach, and he'd pull one of them euc'lyptus cough drops from the general store outa his vest pocket, and stuff it in his cheek. When it'd all dissolved away, he'd shut up. Worked like a charm![1]

Until one Sunday morning, the church-house was fuller than ordinary, ever' pew was a-bulging, and the preacher bounced up to the pulpit, ever' face a-looking at him, smiling in anticipation of a seventeen-minute sermon. He went for the cough drop, and missed. He pulled out a ivory collar button!

Thirty minutes came and went. The flock was a-looking

at their pocket watches in amazement. A hour come and went. The congregation was a-shaking their pocket watches to see if they was broke. The young'uns commenced to squirm, and directly the grown folks commenced to squirm, too.

On their bench at the back, the deacons 'as going mad! They could see them full collection plates jus' a-flying out the winder² on the wings of a dove! They commenced to nudging each other, each deacon hoping one of t'others'd have an idea what to do. The nudging ran clean down the deacon's pew to the eldest deacon, Deacon Smith. Being the eldest, he felt obliged to do something, and the best he could think of was to stand up in the back of the church, look at the preacher, wave his hand a little, and point at his watch.

No good. The preacher was moved by the spirit and kept on a-preaching.

Deacon Smith gave a kind of a jump, waving a little bigger with both arms, and pointed at his watch.

The preacher ignored him.

The deacon was desperate. He reached into the rack on the pew in front of him and grabbed a Broadman hymnal. He r'ared back and throwed the hymnal at the pulpit, hoping to startle the preacher into noticing him.

Well, that there hymnal hit the corner of the pulpit and ricocheted into the air. Jus' at that moment the preacher leaned way back with one hand up toward heaven, and the hymnal just grazed his pompadour. He shucked it off and went on a-preaching.

The missile went on into the choir loft, where it struck the elderly choir leader, a-dozing off in his high-backed chair to the preacher's right.

As the choir leader slid sideways into the carpet, he seen the look on Deacon Smith's face in the back pew, and called out, "Hit me again, Deacon. I can hear the durn fool, and he's still a-preaching!"

[1]Ozarkers put great faith in charms, or good-luck spells and superstitions.
[2]Phonetic for the Ozark pronunciation of *window.*

A fragment of this yarn came from an upstate Missouri informant, but the version shown here is from Informant 8 in 1986. He'd heard it from his father twenty years before.

Duck and Fish

60 **After the preaching, a farmer come** by and invited the preacher-man to come for vittles over to the man's house. He said, "You're right welcome to supper, preacher. We'uns's having duck and fish."

"Well, thanks!" said the preacher, but he couldn't he'p a-thinking what a odd combination that was, duck with fish.

He turned up at the farmer's house a mite later on, and was invited right in to table. The old woman was setting out the food, and all they was was biscuits and gravy.

"Well, it sure looks appetizing, Mis'ress," said the preacher-man, "but did something go wrong? Your husband said we was having duck and fish."

"Tha's it," said the farmer, "duck and fish. Just duck that there biscuit in the gravy . . . then fish 'er out!"

Informant 36 told this one in the summer of 1986. He'd heard it as early as 1930.

Quail-Hunting Mule

There was this feller from the big city, and he loved to hunt quail. But it's real hard keeping a quail-hunting dog in town! So he found this one place where he could hunt, and the woman there kept and rented quail-hunting dogs to city folks. One day, right at the opening of quail season, he drove on out there and said to the woman, "Here I am, and I'd like to rent a quail dog."

"I'm sorry," she said, "I've rented out every single dog I've got today, and I ain't got a one left."

"I drove all this way out here," he said, "and I hate to go back empty-handed. I'd really like to hunt me some quail."

"Well," said the woman, "if you really want to go hunt, I'll tell you what I'll do. For a cut price, I'll rent you my quail-hunting mule."

Now, he saw the mule in the lot, there, and it looked so pitiful; its hip-bones stuck out like a hatrack, its head was drooping down, and its lip was drooping even lower.

"Now, what I am going to do with that mule?"

And she said, "Surprisingly enough, he does a right fine job hunting quail. That's the best I can do; take it or leave it."

He thought about it, and decided he could stand a little embarrassment for some quail hunting, so he took the mule, led it out to the field, unclipped the halter from the lead-rope, and said, "Okay, mule, go get 'em."

I want you to know, that old mule leapt into action: he perked up his ears and just galvanized into a brand-new mule!He started running up the hills, quartering back and forth, working that ground and sniffing for quail! His tail stuck right straight up in the air. He got about halfway up the hill, and he hit a point.[1]

The feller went up there and flushed out the darnedest covey of quail that old mule had pointed up for him, and the mule even hunted down every single bird where they had scattered to. The feller had his limit in an hour.

He led the mule back to the woman and said, "This mule is wonderful! Save him for me next week; I'll be back."

Well, the next week, he came back and took the old mule out and had his limit in a little over an hour.

By the next week, his buddies back in town had begun to think he was out of his mind, bragging on this mule that pointed quail. So they all came out that time, and the feller said to the woman, "I'm here to hunt quail, and I want to rent the mule, and show him off to my friends!"

"Oh, I'm sorry," said the woman. "Ever' single field on this side of the river has already got dogs and hunters in it. There's not a single field on this side of the river for you to hunt in."

"That's all right," said the feller. "We'll go on across the river."

"Oh, no," said the woman. "You'd never get him across the river. He likes fishing even better than he likes to hunt!"

---

[1]Went into the classic pose of hunting dogs in pointing out game to his master.

Informant 26 told this yarn in the summer of 1983. He had heard it in the Illinois Ozarks as early as 1960.

The College Degree

62 **One of those citified college boys** with a degree in something too long to write in the blanks on a marriage license was teasing the locals with some brain-twister math. It started out with, "If a hen and a half lay an egg and a half in a day and a half . . ." and ended up with two-thirds, or five-eighths, or something like that.

Well, he was holding forth in a local drinking establishment, and finally, one of the locals had had too much. He stood up at the table and barked, "If a hen and a half lay an egg and a half in a day and a half, how long does it take a rooster sitting on a sledgehammer to hatch out a hardware store?"

For one blessed minute, the college-educated boy was speechless.

"Give up?" asked the local.

"Yes . . ." said the alumnus.

"So did the rooster!"

Informant 9 says his father told this as a favorite, but what gets sat upon and what gets hatched seem to vary from time to time. He heard it in the early 1960s and has told it ever since.

The Crow and the Prunes

6 3 **Seems there was this little old** woman who decided one day she was going to clean the pantry. She was in there throwing stuff out right and left. You know how you'll have a little bit of something, and you forget about it, and you go out and buy a bunch more of the same thing? Pretty soon you got three or four little pieces of something . . . and you've got to put them all together . . . and make soup? Well, it was that kind of a pantry!

She had 'most everything throwed out, put together, or into the stewpot, when, in the darkest, spider-webbiest corner of that pantry she found . . . a lump.

But she couldn't tell a lump of what.

It was an ol-l-l-l-ld paper bag, with, inside it, kind of moldy and dried up, the ol-l-l-l-ldest, blackest, wrinkled-up-est prunes she'd ever seen in her natural-born life. She walked to the back door and flung them prunes as far as she was able.

While she was in the midst of prune-flinging, this old crow flew through the yard, and was mighty nearly knocked out of the air by the prune bomb.

Well, crows are curious critters, and pretty soon here was the crow, walking around the prune pile, looking it over, tilting his head like a hound dog. He didn't know what they were, but he decided to try one anyway. He picked up one prune in his beak, flew up to the well, set down on the pumphandle, and ate it.

He flew down to the ground, got another prune, flew back up and ate it. He done that about ten times. He was so full, he was about to bust, and was beginning to decide this had not been so good an idea as he had previously thought.

But there was one . . . more . . . prune.

"Now, if I don't eat it," he was a-thinking, "some other crow will get it!"

That done it.

He flew down from the pump handle, waddled over to the prune, ate it, and exploded.

Which just goes to show what your mammy always warned you—don't fly off the handle when you're full of prunes!

Some city people would be baffled by the moral of this tale, if they did not know that "flying off the handle" implies stepping beyond the bounds of sense, and "full of prunes" is a euphemism for being filled with something less appetizing. Informant 38 retold this story from his mother, having learned it around 1970 in Missouri.

The Blacksmith's Revenge

64 **There was this old boy who hung** around town, and went to the blacksmith's every day, just to see what was happening. Every day he asked nosy questions, and he picked up everything and looked at it out of curiosity. One day the blacksmith got weary of the old boy, so he decided to play a trick on him.

He heated up a horseshoe red hot, then doused it quick, and set it out on an anvil just as the old boy was coming into the forge. Sure enough, the old boy picked up the hot shoe to look at it. He set it back down quick! But he didn't say a thing.

"Did it burn you?" asked the blacksmith with a grin. "You set it down awful quick!"

"Nope," said the old boy, "it just doesn't take me very long to look at a horseshoe."

Informant 1 told this story in the winter of 1975. He had first heard it in Oklahoma in the 1920s. The joke is well-known throughout the South and Southwest.

Old Mister Hard Times

6 5 **Old Ma and Old Pa lived up on the** ridge. They was poor, but they got by on almost nothing. Every little bit of extra cash-money they ever got, a penny at a time, went into a baking powder can with a hole cut into the top, up on the fireplace mantel.

A penny here, a penny there, maybe a three-cent nickel now and again. Sometimes Old Ma'd look at 'at can and say, "I sure could use a new housedress."

But Old Pa'd say, "No, no, Ma, Old Mister Hard Times could come at any moment! When 'e gets here, we'll be glad we had our cash money saved."

Later on, Old Ma'd say, "You think if we got into the can—"

But Old Pa'd say, "No, no, Ma! Old Mister Hard Times could come on any day."

Come one day, Old Ma was at the house by herself, and there come a knock at the door. She answered the door, and there stood the worstest-looking little-old beggar-man she'd ever seen in her life. She said, "Who're you?"

And in a scratchy voice he said, "Well, ma'am, I guess you'uns could just call me Mister Hard Times."

She said, "Oh, Mister Hard Times, we been a-waiting for you! I got something for you!" And she ran to the fireplace

and got the Clabber Girl can and give it to him. That was the happiest little old man you ever seen in your life. He plumb skipped down the path as he left. It made 'er heart glad to be making some'un that happy!

Directly Old Pa come home, and she said, "Oh, Pa! It finally happened! Old Mister Hard Times was here, and I give him all that cash-money, and he was the happiest man you ever seen in your life!"

And Old Pa, he musta been happy, too, 'cause he just cried and cried.

This yarn has come from many informants, both as complete stories and as fragments. Informant 31 gave the best rendering in 1983, having heard it from her grandfather twenty years before. The grandfather had known the story "all his life." For a similar theme, see "The Great Hog Meat Swindle," story number 67 in this collection.

Trading for a Mule

So a farmer let out the word that he needed a new mule, and quick as a bobcat, up come a horse trader to his place, leading a mule.

The farmer walked all around that critter, and it sure did look poorly. It was a shade swaybacked and kind of rough-coated; he looked at him from ever' angle. Finally, he grabbed its lip and pulled it up to look at its teeth.

That old mule went crazy. It r'ared right straight up in the air, kicked, bucked, bellowed, all at the same time! It took off like greased lightning and ran smack into the wall of the barn.

The farmer looked at the mule, sitting on its hindquarters with its head a-doddling.

"Dad-gum," said the farmer, angry-like. "I b'lieve that there mule is blind!"

"Blind?" said the horse trader. "Naw—he just don't give a damn!"

Informant 28 told this anecdote in 1983. He has "known this one all his life."

"Come-Heres"

Folks who move into the Ozarks from outside are called "come-heres" by the locals. These tales came here with the come-heres.

The Great Hog Meat Swindle

67 **Onc't a feller went to a hog-scalding** and met the sweetest, dumbest girl he'd ever seen, and married her on the spot. They was home in a soddy[1] when all the meat was smoked, and the feller went out to the smoke house to sort meat. The sweet wife come along, to watch him work. He put all the ribs and the backbone on the west wall, and said, "Them there is for our present need."

"Uh-huh," said the sweet girl, but she didn't un'erstand a word of it.

He put all the shanks and hams on the east wall, and said, "Them there is for the by-and-by."

"Uh-huh."

And he put all the sausage, and the souse, and the bacon on the north wall, and said, "That there is for the afterwards."

"Uh-huh." She took all this in, but she didn't un'erstand a word of it.

The feller said, "I got to ride out a few days. You hold down the fort." He kissed the sweet thing goodbye, and rode out. She swept up and did the chores and was a-setting in the kitchen when up rode a bushwhacker. He was singing a ballad about Price and Snead.[2]

"Pricensnead?" she said to herself. "He's the man the

ribs and backbone's for!" She opened the door. "Are you here from Pricensnead?" she asked him.

Now, the bushwhacker had intended to rob the place, and he was plumb put off by her question. He kind of stammered about and managed a "yes'm!"

"Well," she allowed, "your meat's in the smoke house."

The feller bumbled around, too flusterated to reply.

"I'll get it for you." She went out and lugged back the meat off the west wall in a poke, and give it to him.

Now, this here was the easiest robbery that bushwhacker'd ever come by, and he didn't know much what to make of it.[3] She even slung the poke full of meat onto the back of his horse for him, and said, "If you see Mr. By-'n'-by, tell him his meat's ready, too. But tell him to bring his own poke, I'm all out."

Now, this feller was no fool. He rode hard to the big tree where his henchmen was a-waiting, and emptying out a sack from town. He sent one back to claim he was Mr. By-'n'-by.

Well, in no time a-tall, here rode that second robber with all the shanks and hams. "She told me to look for Mr. Afterwards," he said, so they scrounged around for another sack, and sent the third robber back to the place. They was so took up with how easy this was, they clean forget that it wasn't really pork they had set out to steal that day.

Pretty soon, here comes Mr. Afterwards with the rest of the hog, all smoked up proper-like. Now, they et their fill, then they went off to dig up some gold they'd buried earlier, since their take for the day was all pig meat.

Just then the husband come home, and the wife was so proud of herself. She said, "I gived all the meat to the three fellers you said!"

The feller run out to the smoke house, and stomped around, madder'n hornets. He throwed a ring-tailed fit. Hollered, "We got to find 'em! Smother the fire, and pull the door to!"

Now, he was so flusterated, he took off down the path on foot. The sweet wife ran in and grabbed a rag and wrapped it around the coals in the stove. "Die, you fire!" she hollered, wondering why it was necessary to do that to a fire. Seemed to her like pouring water on it'd've been easier. But she done as she'd been told, and decided to put the rag of coals in the pocket of her apron, and she took off the hinge-straps on the door, and pulled it along behind her, too.

Well, a lot sooner than you'd think, they come to that big tree where the robbers met, and there sat all the meat. But before they could do anything about it, here come them three robbers riding hard. The husband let out a yell, knowing they was cutthroats, and climbed up the tree, fast. The sweet wife just climbed right up beside him, door and all, and sat there and smiled. He just shook his head, and thanked the Lord stupidity wasn't a hanging offense.

The robbers got down, and started pulling money out of their pockets, and emptying their pockets into a pile to divide up all that gold. Now, one of them robbers knowed a lot of scripture, and he laughed and said, "That dumb woman sure repaid evil with good! Like as not, she'd dump coals on our heads!"[4] And he laughed out loud.

Just about that time, the pocket of her apron burned through, and out of that tree come a hail of glowing coals. Needless to say, that set up quite a commotion amongst them robbers, who started jumping around, slapping out their burning shirts.

"It's the Day of Judgment," hollered the little one that knew scripture. "The doors of heaven will open!"[5]

About that time, the door come a-crashing down through the limbs of that tree, and the three bushwhackers took out a-running, and ran till the sun came up the next morning, and was never seen in these parts again.

The husband got on one horse with all the gold, the wife got on another horse, and they tied the door to the other horse and stacked up all the meat on it, rode home, and the sweet wife said, "Honey, it ain't none of my business, but the next time you go to sell meat to somebody, could you maybe have 'em pay in advance?"

---

[1]A sod house.

[2]General Sterling Price and his adjutant, Colonel Thomas Snead, were prominent Confederates on the western border during the Civil War.

[3]He hardly knew what to think of it.

[4]Romans 12:20.

[5]Revelation 4:1.

This Kansas prairie variant paints a pretty picture of the simple wife brought out to a hard frontier life; the Appalachian version, recorded by Richard Chase as "Presentneed, Bymeby and Hereafter," more closely resembles the European original in which the wife and husband are constantly quarreling. Some Ozark versions call this tale "Present Need, By-and-by and Afterwards," since the word *hereafter* almost always refers to the reward in heaven. The inclusion of references to the Civil War and the biblical allusions make this variant unique. Informant 39 related the fragments that make this version different from the Appalachian and European versions. He had heard it in the 1930s and told it in the summer of 1988.

The Old Woman and Her Pig

68 **Onc't upon a time, there was this** old woman lived all by herself at the edge of the woods. One day she decided she was going to do her spring cleaning. Well, she went to sweeping, and mopping, and dusting and waxing, and moving things around—you have to do that when you spring-clean—and she moved this big chair she hardly ever moved, and under that chair was a big, shiny silver dollar. The old woman said, "Mercy sakes! What'll I do with all this money?" (Recollect, this was a long time ago!)

So she said, "I believe tomorrow I'll go to market and get me a pig." And she did.

She went to the market and got the cutest little curly-tailed pink pig you ever saw in your life. She tied a string around its neck and commenced to driving him home.

"C'm'on, pig, le's go home!"

Well, she was doing real good, got almost halfway home, when she come to this stile. She went to trying to get the pig to jump it. He refused.

She said, "C'm'on, pig, le's go!"

"No chance!" grunted the pig.

She tried ever' way she could think of to get the pig to jump that stile. Finally she tied him up to the fence, and left him there, and went off to get herself some he'p.

Well, she went a-walking back along the road a ways, till she come to this hound dog. And she said, "Dog! Dog, bite that pig! Piggy won't jump over the stile, and I ain't going 'o get home tonight."

And you know, that dog wouldn't he'p that old woman. But then she seen this stick alongside of the road, and she said, "Stick! Stick, beat that dog! Dog won't bite pig, piggy won't jump over the stile, and I ain't going 'o get home tonight."

But that there stick didn't stir a-tall, and wouldn't he'p that old woman. But not far along she seen this fire a-burning by the side of the road, and she said, "Fire! Fire, burn that stick! Stick won't beat dog, dog won't bite pig, piggy won't jump over the stile, and I ain't going 'o get home tonight."

And the fire wouldn't do it. Well, poor old woman—but then—she seen this bucket of water, and she said, "Water! Water, quench that fire! Fire won't burn stick, stick won't beat dog, dog won't bite pig, piggy won't jump over the stile, and I ain't going 'o get home tonight."

And the water wouldn't do it, neither. But then, she thought she had it; she seen this great big ox. She said, "Ox! Ox, drink that water! Water won't quench fire, fire won't burn stick, stick won't beat dog, dog won't bite pig, piggy won't jump over the stile, and I ain't going 'o get home tonight."

And the ox shook his head. But then, she knew she had it; she seen this butcher a-coming down the road with his leather apron. You can always tell a butcher a-coming— sometimes with your eyes closed! And she said, "Butcher! Butcher, kill that ox, ox won't drink water, water won't quench fire, fire won't burn stick, stick won't beat dog, dog won't bite pig, piggy won't jump over the stile, and I ain't going 'o get home tonight."

But the butcher refused. Poor little old woman; she was

getting tired! But she went a little fu'ther, 'cause she seen this rope there. And she said, "Rope! Rope, hang that butcher! Butcher won't kill ox, ox won't drink water, water won't quench fire, fire won't burn stick, stick won't beat dog, dog won't bite pig, piggy won't jump over the stile, and I ain't going 'o get home tonight."

But the rope would knot—square knot, granny knot—and the old woman went a little bit further, 'cause she seen this rat. And she said, "Rat! Rat, gnaw that rope! Rope won't hang butcher, butcher won't kill ox, ox won't drink water, water won't quench fire, fire won't burn stick, stick won't beat dog, dog won't bite pig, piggy won't jump over the stile, and I ain't going 'o get home tonight!"

But the rat said, "Naw."

By now, the old woman was plumb tuckered out. So she sat down, and seen this kitty cat, sitting by a barn, all tucked in and purring.

The old woman went over and said, "Kitty cat, will you please go catch the rat, rat won't gnaw rope, rope won't hang butcher, butcher won't kill ox, ox won't drink water, water won't quench fire, fire won't burn stick, stick won't beat dog, dog won't bite pig, piggy won't jump over the stile and I ain't going 'o get home tonight!!"

And the kitty cat said, "Cerrrrrrtainly."

And the old woman said, "You will?"

And the kitty cat said, "I'll be happy to help you with that rat, if you'll go over there to the cow and get me a saucer of milk."

Well, the old woman thought it was the best deal she'd heared so far, so she went to the cow, and she said, "Cow! Cow, will you please gi' me a saucer of milk?"

And the old cow, she said, "Mmmmmighty glad to, if you'll go over to the haystack and get me a' armload of hay."

Well, the old woman she went and climbed the haystack fence, got a big old armload of hay, and took it back to the cow. The cow et it up while the old woman milked a saucerful of milk. She carried it back to the kitty cat, who licked up ever' drop, warshed his whiskers, and then . . .

And then . . .

And then! The cat begun to catch the rat, the rat begun to gnaw the rope, the rope begun to hang the butcher, the butcher begun to kill the ox, the ox begun to drink the water, the water begun to quench the fire, the fire begun to burn the stick, the stick begun to beat the dog, the dog begun to bite the pig, the little pig squ-weeeeealed . . . and jumped completely over the stile!

And you know what?

The old woman got home that night!

According to one source, this is the oldest remaining orally transmitted folk narrative, and it originated in the Middle East, where the old woman went to market to buy a boy slave. The editors have heard it recited, sung to dulcimer music, related in fragments, and told in many variations. Vance Randolph lists a dozen variants in his folk music collection. Informants 1, 2, 5, 6, 24, and 31 have all contributed to this Ozark adaptation.

The Lazy Bride

69 **There was a fine young bachelor** farmer with good bottomland and a fine house and barns. He worked hard, kept his fingernails clean, and was good to his momma—who didn't live with him. But he didn't have a wife, nor any prospects for one. He finally decided to find himself a bride, preferably one who looked like an angel and worked like a mule. He figured she must be out there somewhere, so, one day when all the planting and cultivating was done, he set out wife hunting.

He put on his best Sunday-go-to-meeting suit, hitched the mare to the buggy, and rode three miles to the home of the 'girl next door.' In the course of his courting, he found beautiful girls that were bone-lazy, hard-working young women as ugly as a board fence, but not the girl of his desires. He must have searched for two whole days, and was getting discouraged.

But, as he made for home on the second day, he passed through the village, and saw ... her! She walked like a dream, smiled like a cherub, and dressed like a queen. She turned in at a white-picket-fenced house with lovely gardens, and went inside. He parked his buggy, tied his horse to the fence, and went up to knock on the door.

The young girl's beautiful mother greeted him and invited him in. He honestly announced his intentions, and requested to see her home and her daughter, to see if she would make a suitable wife for a landed gentleman. As they had tea, the ladies looked him over as well. They wanted to see if he could balance a little plate of dainty cookies and a cup of scalding hot tea while making polite conversation, without dropping anything. Well, it was quite obvious that he was a gentleman. And it was quite obvious to him that this home bespoke the lady of his wishes. The house was spotlessly dusted, the dainties were delectable, the linens starched, the curtains ironed, and the floor waxed till it shone. They invited him back to supper, and the repast was excellent; platterful after platterful of old-style cooking. He had asked for her hand in marriage before the dessert even came.

The mother sent the daughter to the kitchen, and spoke with the farmer in private. "I've decided to allow my daughter to marry you, under one condition. You must never strike my daughter in anger."

Why, he could scarcely imagine such a thought, and instantly swore by numerous saints, several of whom he'd never really heard much about, that he would never strike the girl in anger.

The two were wed, the wagon was loaded with the bride's goods, and they made for the farm on the outskirts of town. They got in late that night.

The next morning, he awoke, and there lay his lovely bride with her hair scattered in ringlets and a sunbeam playing on her white skin. He admired her a while, and decided not to wake her. He dressed and went out to milk. He returned shortly, expecting breakfast.

The bride was still asleep, and snoring now. The sunbeam had gone, but the blushing bride was still there.

Deciding she was tired from the excitement of the wedding, he fixed his own breakfast, and went back out to work. He came in when the sun was high, expecting the

first lunch he had not had to prepare for himself since he left his mother's house.

The table was empty, the stove was cold, and the bride was snoring. It didn't take long to figure out the problem—the mother had done all the work in her house! His bride was up two hours that day, demanded that he make some coffee, and was back to bed before sundown.

Well, he hadn't married her for her decorative value. He'd been in mind to get some help around the place! He thought at first that a few gentle hints would do. They didn't. He tried a few frantic comments to make the improvements. They made none. Finally, he got mad. Just when he was about as mad as he could get, he remembered the promise he'd made to her mother.

"I'll have to be smarter than the promise," he said to himself.

The next morning he went out to milk, and left the bride slumbering picturesquely on the pillow-lace. When he returned, he brought a great big tow sack,[1] two sixteen-penny nails, and a claw-hammer. He loudly nailed the sack to the kitchen wall, waking the bride by doing so.

When he had her attention, he announced, "Now, you've been having trouble getting the work done about the house, dear, and I have brought you some help. This sack will be a great help to you, once I've ordered it what to do."

He placed his hands on his hips and commanded the sack to assist his lovely bride in all her chores. Then he went back out to the fields until breakfast time.

When he returned, and there was no breakfast cooked, he loudly scolded the sack. "Sack!" he said. "The stove is cold, the table is empty, and the kitchen is unswept! You'll pay for this!" And with that, he grabbed the sack off the wall and said loudly, "Wife, hold this sack, whilst I pummel it!" And he tied the sack around his bride with its tie-strings, and began to soundly thrash it with the straw-broom. She let out a whoop, and started to run, but

he followed, shouting, "Hold him, dear wife, the lazy var-
mint is trying to escape!" Well, they ran about the parlor,
jumping over chairs for quite a while, until he said, "There,
that should do it! Wife, you've done well!" He returned the
sack to its place on the kitchen wall and said, "Sack, I hope
you've learned your lesson!" And you know, it had. From
that day forward the sack was a perfect housekeeper.

---

[1]Burlap bag.

Informant 43 told this story in 1986. He heard it from his grandmother,
who brought it to the Illinois Ozarks from Poland in the late 1890s. The
story is well-known in Europe, and fit well with the turn-of-the-century
Ozark lifestyle and philosophy. It is apparently told around in Illinois now
as if it had happened there.

The Old Mule Won't Work

70 **There was an old man and his** grandson who lived in an old cabin out in the woods, all by theirselves. The boy was kind of lazy, but he was a good boy. One day the old man said to his grandson, "Go on down there to that barn, and hitch up that old mule, and go plow the north forty."

The boy kind of dragged on down to the barn, and the mule was standing there with his head down in the hay. But he wasn't eating, he was watching the grandson. The grandson come up there, and he said, "Okay, mule, let's go!"

The old mule jerked his head up in the air, and said, "You go and tell your granddaddy that I ain't going 'o work today!"

Well, the boy, he let out a scream and run back up to the house and said, "Granddaddy, Granddaddy, that mule done told me he ain't a-going 'o work today!"

The granddaddy looked at him and said, "You go tell that mule that I said he was going 'o work today."

Well, the grandson, he kind of bit his lip, and gulped a few times, and he went back down there. The old mule was a-watching him real close. The boy got down there and said, "Mule, Granddad said you was going 'o work today."

The old mule threw his head up and kicked around a little bit, and said, "You go and tell your granddaddy I said I wadn't[1] going 'o work today!"

The boy run back up to the house and said, "Granddaddy, that mule says he ain't a-going 'o work today!"

Well, the granddaddy, he's done figured out that the boy, he just doesn't want 'o work. So he says, "Well, I'll go tell that blamed mule myself!" So, he took his cane down off the wall, and he smacked at his little black dog[2] and he hobbled on down the hill to where that mule was, with his grandson a-following behind him a-trembling.

The old man come up close onto the mule; old mule had his head down like he was eating, but he wasn't really. Granddaddy walked right up and rapped the mule on the hoof with that cane and he said, "Now, mule, I said you's going 'o plow!"

That old mule he throwed up his head, and he let out a yowl, and he said, "I told you I wadn't going 'o work today!"

Well, Granddaddy, he let out a scream, and he run just as hard as he could run with his little old black dog behind him. He run, and he run, plumb past the house out into the woods. He found hisself a stump, and he sat down, a-panting hard. He was sitting there, wiping sweat, and the little old black dog ran up next to him.

The man was sitting there, puffing and panting, and he said, "If'n that don't beat all I've ever heard!"

And the little black dog looked up and said, "Yeah, me too!"

---

[1]The contraction *wasn't* comes out *wadn't* when shouted or emphasized in a sentence.

[2]Calling an animal by making kissing sounds with the lips puckered.

Informant 14 told this story in the spring of 1983. Although living in Kansas City, Missouri, he had grown up in the Ozarks. This tale has many variants, including a common barroom joke, but is best known as a story of the African trickster Anansi and his misadventures. Informant 14 learned it from his grandfather in about 1929.

Clever Mollie

7 1 **A rich man had a hill girl for a** maid. Her name was Mollie, and she was smart, but oh, so lazy! One day the rich man called a friend to come to dinner, and he ordered Mollie to make great preparations. She cooked 'em two chickens, one apiece, and the rich man brought a bottle of wine. Then he said, "If only we had finger sandwiches!"

Mollie'd not heared of such a thing, but she said nothing. The rich man went to fetch his friend home, and Mollie set out the plates, and poured the wine. She tasted the wine to see if it was good. She tasted it several times.

Then she tasted the chickens. She tasted on them several times, too. Soon the wine was all gone, and the chickens was bones.

Here come the rich man, putting on airs, bringing his friend along. He set the friend in the parlor and said, "If only we had finger sandwiches!"

He'd just about figured that the wine was gone when Mollie knew she had to think fast. The rich man took out the carving knife to carve on the chickens, and Mollie ran to the parlor and said to the guest, "He's crazy. He's got the knife to cut off your hands and make finger sandwiches!"

Out came the rich man with the knife. The guest hollered out, and ran from the house. Mollie said, "While you was in the kitchen, your guest et one chicken and took the other to home. He drank all the wine, too!"

The rich man ran out with his knife, after the guest, hollering, "Just leave one! Just leave one!"

The guest put his hands in his pockets and hollered out, and ran on, and never saw the rich man again. Mollie laughed, and laughed, and the rich man never knew! Clever Mollie!

Informant 14 told this story in the spring of 1983, and said he'd heard it from his grandfather in about 1929. It is a transplanted Jamaican tale, based on an African Anansi story.

Informants

The stories in this collection have come from some of the many Ozark natives and "come-heres" who have told the authors their varied tales down through the years. The principal informants are briefly described below, to give additional insight into the yarns they spin. Informants' ages are often approximate, and known ages are given as of 1989. No rank or priority is meant in the numbering of the informants, all of whom are rightfully owed the deep respect and gratitude of the authors.

1. Oklahoma-born Missouri grain and cattle farmer of distant Indian ancestry. White male, deceased (1920–1989). (Stories 11, 12, 52, 64, 68)

2. Oklahoma-born Missouri farmwife, widow of Informant 1, of German ancestry. White female, age sixty-nine. (Story 68)

3. Native Oklahoma independent over-the-road trucker, mechanic, and a descendant of Charlemagne. White male, age forty-nine. (Story 58)

4. Texas-born Arkansas college professor with a doctorate in education. White male, deceased (1902–1982). (Story 36)

5. Texas-born Arkansas housewife, widow of Informant 4, of French ancestry. White female, age seventy-seven. (Story 68)

6. Texas-born Arkansas college instructor, with a doctorate in anthropology. White female, age fifty-one. (Stories 4, 67, 68)

7. Native Missourian raised in the country but living in the "big city." White female in her fifties. (Stories 3, 51, 53, 55, 56, 58)

8. Arkansas-born Missouri craftsman and storyteller, blowing

glass in southern Missouri. White male in his forties. (Stories 28, 40, 59)

9. Arkansas-born Missouri craftsman making and selling fine metal products in southern Missouri. White male in his thirties. (Stories 8, 28, 30, 62)

10. Pennsylvania-born retired vaudevillian, storyteller, motion picture and television actor, blacksmithing in southern Missouri, and now you probably know who he is. Old friend of Informant 11. White, male, age seventy-six. (Stories 29, 30, 31)

11. Native Arkansas horse-trader, animal-trainer, craftsman and storyteller. Old friend of Informant 10. White male in his fifties. (Stories 29, 30, 31)

12. Native Missourian, retired sheetmetal shop foreman who took to copper and brassworking later in life. White male, deceased (1929–1988). (Story 23)

13. Native Missourian who works as a chiropractor in a large town, but remembers his country upbringing. White male in his fifties. (Story 20)

14. Native Missourian, born and reared in the Ozarks, now living in Kansas City. Black male in his sixties. (Stories 70, 71)

15. Native Oklahoman from LeFlore County. White male in his forties. (Stories 25, 41, 52)

16. Native Oklahoman from Bartlesville, a country-bred businessman. White male in his fifties. (Stories 21, 45)

17. Native Stone County Missourian, lifelong farmer. White male in his forties. The very first Missourian to share his tales with us. (Story 9)

18. Native Missourian retired coffin-maker from the colorful town of Humansville, now a craftsman and entertainer. White male in his sixties. (Story 33)

19. Native of Harrison, Arkansas. White female, about fifteen years old. (Story 43)

20. Native of Fort Smith, Arkansas. White male in his eighties. (Stories 19, 27, 50)

21. Native Kansas farm wife: a wonderful soft-spoken lady. White and in her seventies. (Story 54)

22. Native Arkansas food-service manager from the Ouachita Mountains. White, male, age thirty-four. (Stories 1, 15, 17, 46, 47, 50)

23. Native Ozark mule-skinner, fast-talking storyteller and pipe smoker. White male in his sixties. (Story 11)

24. Native Missourian. White male in his twenties. He told us

his stories, but nothing about himself. (Stories 1, 3, 20, 22, 26, 68)

25. Native Webster County, Missourian; retired chair caner. White male in his eighties. (Stories 10, 57)

26. Native Illinois farmer and quail hunter. White male in his fifties. (Story 61)

27. Native Missourian from Kansas City, a city kid with a country heart. White female, fourteen years of age. (Story 18)

28. Native Oklahoman from Eufala, just outside the Ozarks. White male in his forties. (Story 66)

29. Native Arkansas farmer and coon-hunter from the town of Bay. A personal friend of the meanest man in Arkansaw. White male, age seventy-eight. (Story 5)

30. Native Arkansas woman. White female in her fifties. (Story 68)

31. Two people: a young married couple, native Missourians from the Sedalia area. White couple in their thirties. (Stories 24, 65, 68)

32. Native Missouri grain farmer, along the Missouri River. White male in his fifties. (Story 32)

33. Native Oklahoman from the Verdigris River area. White male in his forties. (Stories 6, 17)

34. Native Missouri farm wife. White, in her forties. (Story 12)

35. Native Arkansan (that means he was born south of the river) who came to the Ozarks in his teens. White male, age twenty-seven. (Story 48)

36. Native Arkansawyer (that means he was born north of the river), life-long resident of Omaha. White male in his eighties. (Stories 1, 2, 3, 13, 60)

37. Native Missourian, perky white female "over sixty-five, several times." (Story 49)

38. Native Missourian, teenage boy. He didn't tell us anything else. (Story 63)

39. Native Kansas farmer. White, male in middle age. Nothing else was mentioned. (Story 67)

40. Native Missouri seamstress. White female in her thirties. (Stories 16, 35)

41. Arkansas outdoorsman and manager in a nationwide discount-house chain. White male entering his thirties. (Story 37)

42. Native Arkansas farmer in Boone County. White male in his eighties. (Story 44)

43. Native Illinois Ozarker businessman living now in Darien, Illinois. White male in his sixties. (Story 69)

44. Native Arkansas farmwife from Knoxville, Arkansas. White female in her early fifties. (Story 42)

Index of Tales by State

For the more serious storyreaders and storytellers, this index will identify the state in which each tale was collected, or from which each informant identified the tale as coming. Stories that have been heard in more than one state are listed by each state. References are to story numbers.

ARKANSAS: 1, 2, 4, 5, 7, 9, 11, 13, 15, 19, 26, 27, 28, 34, 36, 37, 38, 39, 40, 42, 43, 46, 47, 48, 50, 59, 60, 62, 66, 68

ILLINOIS: 44, 61, 69

KANSAS: 18, 54, 67

MISSOURI: 3, 8, 10, 12, 14, 16, 17, 18, 20, 22, 23, 24, 28, 29, 39, 31, 32, 33, 35, 38, 49, 51, 53, 55, 56, 57, 58, 59, 63, 65, 68, 70, 71

OKLAHOMA: 6, 12, 21, 25, 41, 45, 52, 64

For Further Reading and Arguing

Ozarkers love to argue about stories and word meanings. It's mostly good-natured, and passes many an otherwise lonely hour in a snowbound farmhouse. The attitude is best expressed in an incident that happened to us two decades ago. Asking directions on a particularly narrow and winding set of dirt roads in the Boston Mountains, we were stopped at a shack with a beautiful vegetable garden. The man of the house was hoeing, and we asked him the best road to White Rock. The oldster stood, leaned on his hoe, and opened his mouth to speak. From the porch his wife, seated in a rocker, hollered, "I know a shorter way!"

For those who disagree on the turn of a particular tale, or the usage of a particular word, the editors refer you to these sources of variants on both stories and diction:

Chase, Richard. *The Grandfather Tales.* Cambridge, Massachusetts: Houghton Mifflin Company, Riverside Press, 1948.

———. *The Jack Tales.* Cambridge, Massachusetts: Houghton Mifflin Company, Riverside Press, 1943.

Deane, Ernie. *Ozarks Country.* Branson, Missouri: Ozarks Mountaineer, 1978.

Randolph, Vance. *Down in the Holler.* New York: Columbia University Press, 1953.

———. *The Talking Turtle.* New York: Columbia University Press, 1957.

———. *We Always Lie to Strangers*. New York: Columbia University Press, 1951.

———. *Who Blowed Up the Church House*. New York: Columbia University Press, 1952.

Rayburn, Otto Ernest. *Ozark Country*. Ed. Erskine Caldwell. New York: Duell, Sloan & Pearce, 1941.

Thomas, Roy Edwin. *Popular Folk Dictionary of Ozarks Talk*. Little Rock: Dox Books, 1971.